# LAID TO REST

## The Hopes, Haunts, and Humor
*from My Life Above A Funeral home*

D1714630

## BY
## ROSE GABLER &
## SHEILA LAMB-GABLER

LAID TO REST

*The Hopes, Haunts, and Humors from My Life Above a Funeral Home*

Copyright © 2022 by Rose Gabler and Seheila Lamb-Gabler

Published in the United States of America

*"Death is not the opposite of life, but a part of it."*

-HARUKI MURAKAMI

*This book is dedicated to my family:*
*Michael, Rose, Stephen, Joe, Liz, Matt,*
*and to all of the family and friends who*
*have been Laid to Rest.*

# CONTENTS

# INTRODUCTION

Hello, and welcome to our funeral home. How may we assist you today?

Oh, I'm so sorry for your loss. You're in the right place. Our family has been here to help with these difficult times for over 20 years.

Please, follow me into the arrangement room and we can make sure everything is taken care of for you.

I know these questions are hard, but I'd love to get to know your loved one more. Can you tell me a little about the kind of person they were? What did they enjoy doing? How many family members are there? Spouse? Kids? Grandkids?

Oh, that loud noise? I'm so sorry, that's the Great Dane, Smokey. Yes, we have a few dogs that run around here! More like horses!

He seems to be causing a ruckus out there... I'm sure he'll calm down soon!

Ah, that piercing scream was my daughter, Sheila. I'm sure she's trying to lasso the dog and bring it back upstairs now!

Yes, we live upstairs. It's the easiest commute!

I apologize for the interruption, let me go see if I can assist her quickly so we can continue.

SHEILA!

Dad! I can't get Smokey! He won't come upstairs!

SMOKEY, SIT!

Oh, you got him to sit!

Yes, tell Smokey to sit and he will sit.

Okay, but now how do I get him to move? SMOKEY, MOVE!

No, Sheila, stop yelling. Put his leash on and bring him upstairs. He will follow you with his leash on.

I'm so sorry about the disruption again. Please, let me just review a few of the key points we have discussed.

So, you're looking for a private midnight wake so there is no risk of danger to you or your family members and you're expecting some of the most influential members of your organization from across the country to make an appearance?

Okay, I understand.

This wouldn't by any chance be the Mafia hit from the other day, would it? I thought as much.

Will you be able to provide your own security?

Got it, no problem. We will happily accommodate you. Do you pay cash?

* * *

This was how I grew up. My father and our family owned one of the largest chains of funeral homes in the Midwest and we lived above our flagship on the South Side of Chicago. I was born into a family of embalmers, funeral directors, grave diggers, hearse drivers, and the occasional poltergeist.

I spent my childhood waking up and preparing the chapels, coffee rooms, and lounges for wakes, meetings, and funerals. I would eat breakfast quickly, get ready for Catholic school, and run out the door before returning in the afternoon to do that all again and get ready for the evening or the next day.

I guess you could say I didn't have a normal childhood, although it's the only normal I knew. I can imagine it's similar to growing up on a farm, but instead of tending to crops I was tending to corpses.

While we worked hard, I also learned the importance of playing hard.

As a child in a very serious place, I had my share of fun. Letting the dog out into the funeral home was one of my favorite pranks to play with hundreds of guests in the lobby.

The shrieking, the laughing, the shock, the excitement, it was too tempting!

When I got into high school we had plenty of parties in the chapels and drove hearses filled with kegs of beer to empty cemeteries before school dances. Of course, we were never pulled over. Who would have ever expected a high school girl driving a hearse to be chauffeuring massive amounts of alcohol? Not any cop I knew!

I have been reliving these memories, these eulogies, to my life above a funeral home for years through stories to my children, my friends, and anyone I meet from the South Side of Chicago. However, after all this time I decided to put these stories into writing.

These memories are not just for me, they are for you.

They are for anyone who is grieving.

They are for anyone who feels that they grew up differently from others.

They are for anyone who has trouble finding hope.

This is because living above a funeral home gave me the greatest gift — the gift of living life to the fullest. I immersed myself into each of these experiences as if I was burying a piece of myself with their memories.

And what I have learned is that when something or someone is buried, that doesn't necessarily mean their story is over. It's similar to the quote by renowned artists, Banksy, "I mean, they say you die twice. One time when you stop breathing and a second time, a bit later on, when somebody says your name for the last time."

So, I'm here to bury my stories. Not so that they are over, but so that they are fossilized in history and they can be discovered in future centuries to bring hope and joy to those surrounded by darkness.

However, some of these stories are not solely mine to tell. Therefore, most of the names in this book have been changed. The ones that have remained have given their consent to inclusion in these memories. After all, our parents can't get mad at us now for the things we did back then, can they!? Our children can, but I think they'll be more impressed by our activities than disappointed!

In fact, this brings me to my next point. I haven't written this book alone. This book has been written by me and my daughter, Rose. For months we have discussed, shared, and explored the most meaningful and memorable experiences from my childhood, the ones that seem to stick in everyone's minds and that make the most impact. We have dissected the memories to the tiniest details to be as accurate as possible and to vividly portray the reality of funeral home living, while adding in a little fun.

So, with all of this in mind, I'd like to again welcome you to my life above a funeral home, where all of my memories will finally be. . .

Laid to Rest.

# CHAPTER 1

---

# Get the Door, It's a Corpse

Bong, bong, bong.

*Not again*, I thought to myself as I lay in my bed. I was curled up in my purple comforter and sound asleep when our deep, loud, gong bell rang. It didn't sound like your typical doorbell, and that was on purpose. The gong sound meant that someone was at the backdoor, waiting to deliver. It was Tuesday at 2:07 am, and I was exhausted. I had just gotten back into bed about 40 minutes earlier after the last delivery left, and I wasn't ready. But, there was no one else to open the door. You see, the people who usually accepted these special deliveries only worked until midnight. They would usually call me as they were about to head out, letting me know I was now responsible for what we called "D.B.D." or Dead Body Duty. Since they were gone, it had to be me. I was 17 years old, and I was very tired of being responsible for these deliveries. Every day. Every night. For the past three years.

7

I finally mustered up enough strength to get out of bed when I heard the bell gong again. I must have accidentally fallen back asleep in rebellion. I popped out of bed like a jack-in-the-box on its last turn in my pink curlers, plaid pajamas, thick grey robe, and pink fluffy slippers.

My apartment was at the top of the building, although you could hardly call it a penthouse. I raced through the apartment, down a flight of dark stairs, through a long and dark corridor to the back door.

Each time I did this, I counted the seconds it would take me to reach the back door and always tried to beat my last timing. This activity wasn't only for athleticism purposes; it was first and foremost a solid distraction while darting through this dark, scary building, which only held me and these deliveries.

"Hi Sheila, how are you doing?" said the driver. It was Jeff, the same ambulance driver I had seen just about an hour earlier. He regularly transported bodies from the hospital morgue to the funeral home. Needless to say, we knew each other pretty well.

"Did you go right back to sleep when I last came, or did you stay up and eat?"

I was a great one for snacking during the night. I still am today.

"I went to sleep. . . I see you have another one for me."

"I do. Do you need help bringing it in?"

"No thanks, I can do it. They won't let you off just yet, huh?"

"Not yet, Sheila. Maybe after this one."

As I signed for the delivery, Jeff reminded me that the night was just beginning.

"Well, if I don't see you again tonight, say hi to your family."

I sarcastically laughed as I rolled my eyes. I figured I would probably see Jeff again shortly and I became exhausted thinking that I would never be able to get a whole night's sleep in this building.

As I began to roll the cold silver gurney down the hall, I noticed it seemed heavier than usual, and I wasn't sure exactly why. I didn't care to know, either. I knew if I did, I would be having nightmares about it. I definitely wouldn't get any rest, then.

Down the hall, not too far from the back door, was the commercial elevator. It was ancient. It was one of those terrifying transporters you had to lock yourself in and wait for the massive steel door to shut in place before you would start to move automatically.

I pushed the delivery into the elevator that fit just about the length of a gurney and the width plus one person to operate the movement. I slid into the side and closed the folding gate.

It was just me and the corpse in the elevator now. However, in order to emotionally detach myself from this procedure, I would try to forget the fact that there was a dead body next to me. There's something incredibly unnerving about being so close to death, and it wasn't until I got much older that I realized how beautiful these moments could be, as well. But, more on that later.

Once the folding gate clicked closed, the steel door automatically shut. There were only two buttons in this elevator, up and down. I pushed the cold, smooth "down" button. There was a quick jolt, and then it slowly moved.

Through its small window, I saw the cinder blocks that made up the foundation of the building. As I watched that view, lots of ideas ran through my head. Mainly, I hoped that this delivery wouldn't move, as they had a few times before. Once we arrived at the basement, I reached the other side of the elevator to open the folding gate and then waited for the creepy steel door to open fully.

During these moments is when I would sometimes go into full panic mode. This immense feeling of dread would creep inside my heart as the door always took a few moments too long to open. I could even feel the goosebumps begin to swell across my body. I would try to get the gurney out of the elevator repeatedly before the door were completely open, hoping that I wouldn't scare myself with the banging noises against the folding door, I would say to myself; *we're almost there, we're almost there.* Sometimes, I would even scream it to myself just to hear my voice above the chaotic energy rushing through my mind.

After all of the deliveries I had received over the past few years, you'd think that I would be able to do this with ease.

While some days felt easier than others, I'll tell you one thing — I never got that comfortable.

Tonight felt different, though. It felt more intense for some reason. Like I was not only shuffling inventory but that there was something else with me. I felt as if I was being watched. Followed. Stalked, even. I guess I was more tired than I thought tonight because the more aware of my exhaustion I became, the more terrified I was.

When I finally exited the elevator, I wheeled the gurney into the ice-cold room at the end of the hallway and turned on the light. Looking around the room, I remembered I had already received one delivery earlier in the night. I gently pushed it to the side and moved the new delivery in. The cooler could hold about ten of these deliveries, so it was always like playing a game of Tetris to get them to fit.

This moment is where music would play a valuable role. I would sing songs to distract myself from my surroundings or maybe make up rhymes and poems. Sometimes I prayed, and other times I would repeat the Alphabet over and over. As I grew older, I would even say it backward. I would go to extreme measures to numb myself to the emotions that were present in that room.

Once I settled everything and had the two gurneys safely secured in place, I felt an immediate sense of relief knowing I could get back in bed. I turned around and shut off the lights. I quickly skipped back over to the elevator, humming a tune and psyching myself up for another elevator ride.

I always loved the feeling of pushing the "up" button. Even though I could still see the cinder blocks through the window, I always felt as if I was rising from the grave and welcoming new life. Cue "Lion King" intro song, "The Circle of Life".

This moment is when I would feel comfortable enough to ponder what kind of life each body had lived. I would focus on how much it meant to others and ask questions like:

Did they make people happy?

How many people would turn up in a few days to view them?

What kind of journey had they been on?

I would often hope the best for each body that I shuffled to the basement, believing in the best that they could have been. Of course, they made everyone around them happy, and hundreds of people would swarm around their casket in tears for their loss. The adventures across the globe they had experienced and with their family and friends locally would live on in memories forever.

The elevator eventually stopped as it arrived at the main floor. I pulled open the squeaky folding gate and waited for that all too slow steel door to open. Feeling a bit of desperation to get back to sleep, I squeezed myself through a small crack just as the door was beginning to open. I tore through the double door that led me back into the main corridor and ran as fast as I could up the stairs. I pushed open the big wooden door to my apartment, which was a bastion to protect me from the delivery process.

I had finally crossed the finish line!

As I jumped back into bed, I took a second to make sure I didn't lose a curler during this episode. Even if I had lost one, there were rarely any nights where I would want to go back downstairs and look for it.

If I was tired enough I would fall right back to sleep, but other times I would frighten myself thinking about where my bed was. See, my bed was located in the apartment at the top of the building, precisely two floors above that chilling storage room. The deliveries were just two short flights away, and between our floors was a large room where we would hold the viewings for the wakes and funerals.

This scared me because I would have nightmares that I would wake up and not be in my bed or on my floor at all. I would sometimes sit up and look out at a sea of empty chairs. It would take me a moment to look down, but I would eventually discover that even though I was wrapped in my purple comforter with yellow flowers, I was in a dark brown casket, surrounded by bright white pillows just one floor below. In other dreams I would sit up, freezing, in a dark room, and feel my legs under a cold zipper encased in a bodybag two floors down.

Sometimes the only thing that would wake me up from these nightmares was the gong for the D.B.D. but that didn't mean relief from my nightmares. It meant I would also wake up knowing I would have to face the fears that plagued my dreams.

While there were only two bodies that came in so far that night, sometimes we would receive the full ten. This was because even though we had several of these funeral homes in the Midwest area, many of them weren't fully equipped. Our location had the largest embalming room, making it the first stop from the hospital before dispersing to any one of our family's funeral homes. Everything and everyone was transported through this one. Our main one. My family's home.

I would go back and forth between feeling relieved to have woken up from those nightmares and anxious to receive the next body from the back door. I would have to remind myself that this funeral home wasn't just my house, it was also the first restful space for the dead.

When I would take in these bodies I was always nervous that one would start releasing air, or even sitting up while we were alone, which can happen for hours after death because of muscle spasms. I also often scared myself into thinking I could see and hear their spirits following their bodies along this journey until they were laid to their final resting place, which explained the feelings of being stalked throughout the night.

These thoughts horrified me as I would run through the funeral home back and forth from our apartment to the embalming room every night.

My bed was the only space that was truly mine in the whole 15,000 square foot building and I would do anything to stay there as long as possible and get back as quickly as I could. And that was usually only if our Great Dane, Smokey, would let me in the bed. He seemed to feel the same way about my bed as I did. Fifteen thousand square feet for his 120-pound body to roam, and his favorite place was in my small twin-sized bed with me. Even though it was quite a tight fit, his presence gave me comfort. I knew I had a warm body sleeping next to me to keep me safe. If anything was going to come into my room, or if I was going to fall down a floor or two, Smokey would let me know.

My bed was my haven. I witnessed the best and the worst of life from this little space as I was surrounded by my flower power wallpaper, my countless "Groovy" posters that adorned the walls, and smothered by my Great Dane.

The life I experienced living in an environment of death would define me in ways I would never have imagined. Along with inspiring my life's journey in ways that I most definitely hoped for.

# CHAPTER 2

---

# Vampire, Ghost, or Brother?

I'm sure you can imagine - people had a lot of questions when they learned I lived above a funeral home.

My friends, my friend's parents, my friend's grandparents, my neighbors, my friend's neighbors, my teachers, the deli workers, the gas station attendants (especially when we were in a hearse) or anyone I generally came across.

One of the many questions I would be asked out of many was: "Sheila, what does your home smell like?"

While our apartment smelled pretty normal from homemade food, big smelly dogs, and always a lot of laundry to do, they would usually get a little more specific.

"Does your house smell like flowers? Or formaldehyde?"

I would always answer matter-of-factly. "Well, the chapel and the florist on site smells like flowers, and the embalming room smells of formaldehyde. But they're not in my home. They're in different parts of the building."

I would be rolling my eyes in my head, duh. Who do you think we are? The Addams Family? *Snap snap.*

Another obvious question I would get was "Do you hear things in the night, like ghosts?"

That one was a little more difficult to answer. I didn't want my friends to be scared to come over, nor did I want their parents to think it wasn't safe. I usually just laughed and moved on, while trying to avoid the question all together.

While the people who lived in normal homes may have found it super-eerie to live above a funeral home, it was a lot of fun for my brother, Matt, and I! You see, we LOVE scary movies. Anything that had supernatural terror linked to it, we would watch it.

I remember when Dracula, The Werewolf, and Frankenstein were all the rage in scary movies. At night, my parents would always be in the office, talking to people, and "working the wakes," as we called it, which meant showing their faces and expressing their condolences to as many people as they could to show how far our services would go. They usually wouldn't finish their day until 11:00 PM or later. They were also very socially active, always attending fundraisers and black tie functions at night. That left a lot of nights where Matt and I would be home alone. And nothing makes a scary movie scarier than being home alone.

Matt would turn all the lights off and we would pop popcorn, grab blankets to hide under when we were frightened and sit directly in front of the TV. I was the worst person to watch a scary movie with because before it even started I would be shaking in fear and once the movie started, I was absolutely petrified!

My brother loved how scared I got, and how gullible I was. He would take full advantage of that when we were home alone. Often, Matt would try to play horrifying pranks on me. One time he went to the bathroom and came back dressed as Dracula! He had gotten the fangs after school, put on my mom's makeup to make him look pale, used ketchup as blood, slicked his hair back with gel, and wrapped himself in a black cape! He walked out of the bathroom with one arm covering his mouth just as Dracula would sneak up on his prey. And then he would extend his other arm out and mimic Dracula's deep voice and motion for me to "Come closer!" Those two words with his costume would put me directly over the edge! I would scream at the top of my lungs, run past him as fast as I could, and slam my bedroom door behind me, still screaming! Sometimes, if his costume was particularly good, I wouldn't even risk staying the in the apartment! I would run downstairs to the funeral home and hide in a chapel until Matt finally assured me that Dracula was gone.

I remember one time when I was 10 years old I ran downstairs in my pajamas and found a manager still working late one evening. I darted to her desk and screamed in complete fright: "Dracula is here! He's here! He wants my blood! He'll drink all of our blood!"

It turned out that there was still a funeral in progress. Everyone who was mourning turned and looked at me as if I was completely out of my mind.

My mom ran across the chapel and into the office. She grabbed me by the arm into my father's office and held me to calm me down.

"Sheila, what's wrong?" she gently asked as I started to relax a little.

I was still crying, but I quietly whispered, "Dracula is upstairs."

She sternly told me to stop and explained it was my brother, Matt, teasing me again.

"I don't care, I am not going back upstairs without you!"

"Well, I am not going back upstairs for a while. You can quietly wait here if you want to wait for me."

I sat there quietly for the rest of the night in my pajamas. It was hours before my mom and dad were finally ready to go upstairs.

When we went upstairs Matt was waiting for me with a string of garlic. He felt bad that I had gotten so scared and wanted to protect me from the vampires.

"Sheila, I saw in the film that vampires don't like garlic. Keep this with you and you'll be safe."

I went to bed holding onto that string of garlic tightly, but didn't feel it was enough.

I went to the grocery store the next day and bought loads of garlic and made multiple strands of garlic necklaces. I wore those smelly strands for months! And if I wasn't wearing it, it was hanging on my headboard. I even hung it on my bedpost while I was at school to make sure the scent stayed around my bed at all times. There was no way that a vampire was going to get anywhere near me or my bed! Even if the vampire was my brother. How did I know if Matt was or wasn't one after all!? I wasn't going to take that risk!

I remember a few weeks after wearing this braid of garlic I overheard my teachers talking about how they smelled garlic often lately and wondered where it came from. I giggled but, ultimately, felt safe that garlic could be smelled around me everywhere! I knew I was protected and that I was protecting others, as well!

However, watching scary movies wasn't the only way that we enjoyed spending our nights alone at the funeral home. There were plenty of other ways that we paralyzed one another with fear.

When you think of old-school seances, what probably comes to mind is a woman wearing a scarf around her head sitting at a round table in front of a glowing orb as she conjures spirits and speaks to the dead. While my experiences weren't this elaborate, they were always eventful.

I did seances with Matt for years. As you can probably tell, he was a few years older and always knew exactly how to instill me with fear and excitement at the same time.

Whenever we had friends over, this was the entertainment of choice. Late-night seances in the funeral home. Fun, right? My brother was always the ringleader of our haunted evenings. Matt could set the scene perfectly for an eerie night in one of the funeral home wake rooms. As if every night wasn't creepy enough, Matt was a professional fear master.

Matt would lead all of us downstairs, whether there were five of us or fifteen of us, it didn't matter, he was always prepared to guide us through a spiritual journey. When we would reach the lobby, we would all gather candles from around the building and bring them to one of the chapels.

We would hand them to Matt and as he arranged them, he would ask everyone to sit in a circle. Then he would direct us to all hold hands.

Once we were settled and all grasping one another hands, Matt would look at us all straight in the eyes, as if he was peering into our souls, and make us swear that we wouldn't let go of each other no matter what happened. We would each agree, shake our heads, and watch as he moved on to the next person and the next. He would then light the candles and respectfully reach out to the spirits.

"Spirits, we come in peace. We want to talk to you, we want to know how you died, and we want to see if you are happy now. If there are any spirits here, we ask that you give us some kind of a sign that you are present."

We would sit with our mouths shut so we wouldn't breathe too loud and gaze around the dark room, looking for any sign of movement outside of our little circle. There were no windows in the funeral home chapels, so these rooms were pitch black when the door were shut and all of the lights off. As the silence grew, we would either begin shaking or become completely frozen and petrified. We would hope not to hear or see anything but also secretly wanting to have an experience. The littlest things would make us scream, like the air conditioning kicking on, or the heat, or a honk of a car outside. We would do this for hours, never letting go and never chickening out.

Years went by and our seances began to fizzle as my brother moved out and rarely came home from college. My parents had moved to the city and I was living alone above the funeral home at this point. My girlfriends were my family, and they stayed over often. But I'll never forget of the most terrifying experiences of my life.

A group of my girlfriends were over for the night and we decided to do a seance. My brother suggested we do it properly, with the same procedure that we did when we were younger in hopes that we would be able to communicate with the same spirits from before. We agreed to go that route as we had all done it before. Matt asked us to gather the candles and matches and to meet him in the chapel. We grabbed all of the candles we could find and sat in a circle holding hands as we had many times before.

He began the session by asking us all to promise, once more, that we wouldn't let go of one another's hands, no matter what happened. We each agreed. This little, intimate, terrifying moment certainly did build up the anticipation of the seance and prepared us to expect fear.

My brother began to speak to the spirits once again.

"We would like to make contact with any spirits here. Please make yourself known."

We sat in silence, waiting for the next few moments to pass. The same feeling rose inside my gut. I was hoping to hear a quick knock, while also praying I didn't hear anything.

We began to hear faint whispers surrounding us. Brief noises that weren't coming from any of us. We began to shush one another to try to understand what was being softly mumbled.

I gasped as I understood the voice. My friends did as well.

We clearly heard it say my name.

The voice slowly and quietly hissed "Sheila. . ." I began to shake uncontrollably as everyone turned and looked at me in disbelief at what we had just heard.

We remained silent for a few moments before I finally built up the courage to answer.

"Y-Yes?" I quietly stuttered.

After a few moments, we heard another name.

"Julie. . ."

Her name was drawn out as if there were five u's in her name. Juuuuulie.

She grabbed my hand so tight I thought it was going to break.

"Did you just hear my name, too?" She frantically asked.

We all shook our heads, again, in total disbelief.

Out of all of these years of seances, we had never heard words. Only sounds. I began to think this must be the spirits finally communicating with us after seeing us for so many years.

That thought quickly dissipated as we heard another name.

This time, it was Grace's turn.

She looked at each of us and bit her lips together so that she couldn't let out her fear. In the candlelight, it looked as if her lips were beginning to turn purple from biting them so hard.

As we were shaking my brother reminded us that we had made a pact, a promise, not to break the circle. He told us that if we opened the circle we might let free whatever was speaking with us, and without knowing more about it, we could let destruction loose in the funeral home.

Grace and Julie began to quietly sob, asking to close the seance so they could go home. They didn't want to be here any longer, and I didn't blame them, I prayed that I could leave, too. How did we know we didn't already let something loose? How could our circle keep a spirit contained? Especially as we were hearing it all around us.

I began to yell at my brother, asking him to tell us how to make it stop.

As I began yelling, the voice did, too.

"SHEILA! JULIE! GRACE!"

And this time, he added a name.

"MATTHEW!"

One more time, he yelled all of our names.

"SHEILA! JULIE! GRACE! MATTHEW!"

His voice sounded like a deep growl at this point. It kept getting deeper, darker, and louder each time he said our names. We were in tears and looking all around the room for the source of the voice that was surrounding us.

"SHEILA! JULIE! GRACE! MATTHEW! I'M GOING TO GET YOU, AND WHEN I GET YOU. . . I AM GOING TO EAT YOU!" Followed by the darkest, most sinister laughter you have ever heard.

That was enough for us! We darted out of that room faster than rockets, screeching and sobbing looking for the closest phone. We were bumping into one another as we were looking in the dark. We were yelling to each other to call someone when we found a phone. We needed someone to pick us up. One of our friends or their parents had to come and pick us up, and we had to leave immediately.

That's when I turned and looked at my brother, who was laughing uncontrollably. He pointed over to the front office and under the faint red light of the "EXIT" sign, we saw a body-like figure crawling through the doorway making obscene noises.

At this point, we were almost wetting our pants in fear. I grabbed my friends because they were frozen in their place, scared to move, and dragged them through the funeral home lobby, towards the back door, and out into the parking lot. We hugged each other as we cried and vowed to never host another seance again.

Just then, the door slowly began to open and we were terrified at what could possibly be coming. My brother slithered out of the doorway with a massive smile on his face, and he was followed by his friend, John, who could not contain his laughter.

It was then that I had realized John was the voice. He was the one speaking over the intercom system the whole time. It was a system we only used for music during wakes and funerals, but it also had a microphone in case of emergencies, but we had never used it for that purpose, so I had never heard anyone speak through it. My brother asked his friend to come over earlier before we began the seance so that he could teach John how to use the speaker system. They planned the pauses, the names, the laughter, the whole bit.

We were absolutely furious! We took turns hitting each of them as we were screaming our anger.

"ARE YOU CRAZY?!" We were pissed. No, pissed was an understatement! We were absolutely furious!

I don't think I had ever been so upset with my brother. Even if it is hilarious to think about all of these years later. It was rather clever. And we were truly terrified.

I can't stop laughing now as I think about it.

My friends were still so angry that they wanted to leave. Grace went back inside and called her dad to come and pick us up. We went to her house and left everything in the apartment upstairs. Matt and John stayed at home that night, but we didn't have any clothes, sleeping bags, or necessities for a sleepover as we were too angry, and still a little too scared, to stay inside.

The next day, we went back to my apartment, and Grace and Julie gathered their things. They didn't stay over again for a very, very long time!

The lengths Matt went to were unimaginable for a teenager! And the level of fear I already felt in general showcased that I didn't need much convincing that something scary was going on! To say I was traumatized by him, and still experience PTSD from his pranks to this day, is an understatement. If one of my children walks into the kitchen without me knowing and says one word I leap across the room in terror and scream at them!

"YOU HAD NO IDEA WHAT I HAD TO GROW UP WITH! THIS IS UNACCEPTABLE! MAKE YOUR PRESENCE KNOWN WHEN YOU ENTER A ROOM!"

Usually by the time I have made the leap they are already in tears from laughter. I have to say, when I get them back though, I laugh just as hard! Ah, sweet, sweet, revenge, we meet at last! While it's 26 years after the fact, it is still a delectable feeling!

# CHAPTER 3

———

# Comforting the Cardinal

When a high-ranking member of the Catholic church passed away, the whole town shut down. Stores close, restaurants close, schools close, everyone stays at home and is expected to pray for the deceased. While the whole town is eerily quiet, that usually meant our family were going absolutely mad.

This was one of my first high-profile funeral experiences, when a local Chicago-based Cardinal passed. I was fifteen years old, and I will never forget it.

My father woke me up on the morning of the wake at the break of dawn. Even though everyone was supposed to be mourning and praying, I wasn't allowed a moment to myself to even process what was about to happen.

"Sheila, you have a few big jobs to do today, and I need you to get up and get ready now! Meet me in my office when you're done."

"Okay, Dad."

I slowly dragged myself out of bed and when I went into the kitchen I could hear the commotion outside and in the lobby downstairs. It sounded like a shopping mall on Black Friday with hundreds of people running around, chattering about everything, yelling occasionally, and going completely insane over the biggest and best sale. The emotions were so intense I could feel the chaos in the air.

I looked out the front windows and saw news trucks and camera crews everywhere! There were police cars with their lights on blocking the streets in every direction. Everyone was acting erratically. I had never seen so many things happening simultaneously for a death and I began to get more and more excited about having a few "big jobs" as my dad had mentioned!

I rushed to the shower, grabbed my black uniform, and darted down the stairs ready to take action for the day! I couldn't wait to hear how I would be participating.

I weaved my way in and out of all of the people, the camera crews, the journalists, the funeral directors, the florists, and more and finally made it to my father's office. He was having a meeting with the managers of the funeral home, and the executives of the news stations. They were all reviewing the plans for the day. It became apparent to me that he was in charge of this whole event. And that's what it was, an event. It was so much more than the usual wakes and funerals we were used to, or even the abnormal wakes and funerals we were used to.

He was directing where the cameras would be for the services, where the funeral directors would stand, how the processional would progress. The whole enchilada. It sounded intense and I continually got more and more excited about my part in this day. I was the funeral owner's daughter, and he was in charge of everything. Was I going to be his right-hand man? I hoped so! I wanted a piece of all of the action!

When the meeting faded, I went up to my dad's desk.

He sat in his chair and sighed a bit of relief for a moment.

"Sheila, today is a big day. One of our biggest days, and I need your help. "

"Anything, Dad!"

"I need you to be in charge of the walkie-talkies and my coat."

"What?!"

"We're all going to be communicating with walkie-talkies today so we can make sure everything goes perfectly, but they're not ours and we have to return them. So I need you to make sure everyone keeps track of their walkie-talkie."

"And your coat?"

"I don't know if it's going to be chilly or not, so I'd like to have it nearby if I do need it."

Just then, my father was called away to answer some questions.

I sat in a chair, completely disappointed. I didn't want to babysit the walkie-talkies. Such an annoying job. I rolled my eyes looking at them, but did as my father asked.

Soon after our chat, funeral directors, news station executives, police chiefs, and anyone else my father told to grab a walkie-talkie stopped into his office to pick theirs up. I had no clue as to who I was supposed to expect next. There was no list of walkie-talkie permits, or extra batteries to be seen. Whoever got to my station first was given walkie-talkie and the rest were on their own.

Once everyone was prepared, my father came in and grabbed one of the last three we had. I picked up the last two and we all headed to our cars. We had to be at the church early to prepare for the wake that was about to begin.

I picked up one of the Cardinal's prayer cards on the way out and noticed that his death date was three days before this day. I was shocked that all of this was able to be done so quickly.

Usually, there's about a week of time when all of the plans for a wake and funeral to come together. I thought to myself this must be standard procedure, or maybe they knew that the Cardinal was going to die soon. I decided to inquire further.

I was riding over to the church with my father and asked him how this all came together so quickly.

"We have no choice, Sheila. Catholic clergymen aren't treated the same way as everyone else when they die. They must be buried as soon as possible out of respect."

I was surprised. I didn't understand what the difference was, but assumed it had to do with the smell or the look of a dead body.

"Can I sit in the back of the church?"

My father smiled a little and said "Sure. You have a walkie-talkie too, so if you need anything just turn it on and to channel four. We're all on there and can hear what you say, so only use it for emergencies."

I nodded my head.

"This service is invitation only, so we shouldn't have any problems. But just in case, you know how to get ahold of someone if you can't see anyone."

I sat in silence for a moment and started imagining how the rest of the day would go. More and more questions began to pop up in my mind, and I decided to keep asking them. "What about the casket? Did we have one ready?"

My father looked over at me somewhat shocked. I think he was impressed and confused by the fact that I knew the expected timeframe for caskets. Especially the special order caskets, which I assumed this one was with all of the hubbub happening.

"It was a bit of a rush this time, but the casket makers got it done just in time. They delivered it late last night."

"Oh good," I said in a professional manner. Yes, father, I knew what I was talking about!

A few minutes later we arrived at the church. I sat down in the last pew and watched everyone running in circles around me. The door to the church were closed and I could hear hoards of people chattering outside waiting to be let in.

My father directed the cameras to go to the second floor of the church and set up there. The views were better, and their distance was respectful to the deceased, and not to mention the few visitors who appreciated their privacy.

He instructed the funeral directors to stand in the corners of the room and help direct the visitors as they were walking through the church, past the casket, and then guide them to their seats.

Then he got everyone's attention:

"EVERYBODY! The doors are about to open. When they do, we will be silent. If there are any issues, use your walkie-talkies. Although, we should not have any problems that we cannot handle throughout this day, and if we do, you can bet one of you will be the next one in a casket!"

Everyone went silent.

My father waved at the cameras and counted them down to go live.

Mouthing the numbers and using his right hand he motioned "Three, two, one" and then did a thumbs up. The red lights on the cameras turned on, and the show was about to begin!

He moved to the front of the room and stood at the end of the casket while two other funeral directors stood guard in front of the casket to ensure there weren't too many people surrounding the Cardinal at once.

The first ones through the door were the Bishops, Cardinals, and Priests who were visiting from across the country to pay their respects. My father stood to the side of the front and greeted each of them as they passed by before heading to their seats.

I watched as one of the first Bishops who passed by the casket grabbed my father's arm and invited him to talk further off to the side. I saw him motioning with his hands up and down but couldn't understand what he was saying.

I decided to turn on my walkie-talkie to see if anything was being said about their conversation.

After a few more seconds of talking, my father shook his head and then shook the Bishop'shand  and directed him to the pews. Then he reached for his walkie-talkie and headed towards the back of the church. "Funeral directors except for the two by the casket, head to the back, NOW!"

Quickly, all of the funeral directors made their way to the back of the church.

They all gathered behind me in the corner so I turned off my walkie-talkie and turned my head a bit to try and hear what was going on.

"The Cardinal's feet are too high. The Bishop that just pulled me aside told me that the Cardinal's feet cannot be higher than his head, and saw that there is a zipper where we can remove some of the stuffing. So we're all going to go up, pay our respects, unzip the cushion and pull out some of the stuffing. Shove it in your pockets and then make your way back here to throw it out. Got it?" They all nodded in agreement.

The funeral directors then stopped the Bishops, Cardinals, and Priests and cut in line to pay their respects, and to pull out the stuffing.

My father was the first one to the front with two other funeral directors. They made the sign of the cross and one of the managers slowly reached in to unzip the cushion so they could begin pulling out the stuffing. But before he managed to unzip it enough, the zipper busted and white stuff came flying out everywhere!

You could hear them all gasp together and race to pick up the mess!

My father turned around and motioned to the cameras to turn their cameras away from the casket. The funeral directors, Cardinals, Bishops, and Priests that were near the front all scrambled to the casket and began picking up the chaotic mess that just exploded across the front of the church. The cushion had been so overstuffed that it couldn't keep in barely anything when that zipper opened.

Everyone that was carrying the white mess then escaped out into the hallway.

I quickly turned on my walkie-talkie to see if I could overhear anything happening.

I heard my father's voice "Everyone act normal as you head to the front of the room again, but look around the floors and the front pews, and everywhere surrounding the casket, even in the casket, the filling is made of Kotex pads!"

He left his walkie-talkie in talk mode and I heard Clergymen questioning my father.

"Why is the Cardinal's cushion filled with Kotex Pads?! I've never touched one of these before in my life!"

I ran out to the hallway and spied on them with the volume down as low as it could be so I could still hear what they were saying.

Then another Cardinal yelped "Are they used?!"

Upon further inspection they agreed, they had not been used.

"How do we fix this?!" A Bishop howled as he pulled out a cigarette and lit it in the hallway.

During all of the commotion I saw a Cardinal run into the bathroom and he quickly darted back out moments later with wet towels for everyone, they were wiping their hands to clean them off and wiping their foreheads from the stress.

"I'm not sure Bishop, but it's not something I can fix now, or maybe ever! Get back out there and mourn the Cardinal, I will take care of the cleaning up!"

The Cardinals all returned to their seats and the funeral continued without any further distractions, hiccups, or stuffing.

However, there was never an opportunity to switch the stuffing.

My father left the funeral, got into his limo, and instantly called the owner of the casket company, Fred.

"What do you mean you ran out of cushion filling, Fred?!"

I could see my father's face turning red with anger, or maybe it was embarrassment. Probably a little bit of both.

"The next time you run out of filling for a casket, especially a casket for a Catholic Cardinal that is going to be televised, you tell me! Don't just send your daughter to the grocery store to find out what kind of white fluffy crap you can use! I could have swapped the cushions with another casket! Now the Cardinal is going to be buried on Kotex pads and the whole VATICAN knows!"

That Cardinal is still buried with a bed of pads to this day.

At least he can rest assured that everything is being absorbed!

# CHAPTER 4

---

# Who Needs The Plaza?

Growing up on the south side of Chicago, I knew my family was different.

We used to play hide and seek in the casket rooms, in the embalming rooms, and even in the body bags. The visiting rooms were my personal playgrounds, but my favorite space was in the basement. We had a massive room in the basement that was called the Community Room.

This room was available for anyone in the community who needed a larger space for meetings, parties, family gatherings, etc. We could make that room into anything. We did so well that The VFW would meet there instead of using their local halls!

While it was a great space for these purposes, it was also my personal skating rink. I would often go down there and tie my skates over my shoes before rolling quickly to the other side. When I would bring friends over, they would get their skates and go around that room for hours. We would race to see who could bang on the paneled walls across the room first. After a while, I got really good. I could skate backward, and I learned how to skate leg over the leg and with a partner, all with my old, tattered shoe skates. My parents noticed how often I was skating and got me real four-wheeled roller skates! I thought to myself, "I'm in the big leagues now!" I continued to skate. I skated until that pair became even more tattered than the first pair.

While you may be thinking, this is so cool! That isn't even the best part of living above a funeral home. Like the hit movie series *Eloise* who ruled over The Plaza Hotel, I was the Princess of the flagship funeral home and everyone who worked there loved me. Walking down the halls, everyone would greet me as if I were their superior.

"How's your day going, Ms. Lamb?"

"You look lovely today, Ms. Lamb! Is that a new school uniform?"

"Do you need help with your homework today, Ms. Lamb?"

"It's great to see you up and about, Ms. Lamb!"

Yep. They all loved me, and I loved being around them. Little did they know, but I thought of a lot of them as if they were family. It was like having fifty parents! It may sound overwhelming, but I loved having such a big community. I never felt alone. Especially as the years went on and I took on new roles in the business, they were always happy to lend a hand and guide me. Living in the same building that you work in allows you to build unique bonds with the other people who work there. It also presented an intimate opportunity to involve ourselves in our customers' lives to new extents.

When our customers would walk through the front door of the funeral home, it was as if they were walking into our private living room. We were always welcoming everyone into our home, customers, strangers, friends, and family alike. It was unlike any other business that I had experienced. However, it's because of this welcoming atmosphere that I have always enjoyed having a revolving door in my home. I have always enjoyed hosting people and planning celebrations. I've gotten good at it over the years, and it's because of the pressure I felt to be good at it when I was younger.

You see, my parents went above and beyond when it came to serving the families who were having wakes in our building. The process would begin with the family visiting one of our funeral homes and meeting with a director to plan the services in a way that would respect the deceased. These preliminary discussions usually took a few hours, so our family and our team would get to know the families very well during emotional times. Death is such a fragile experience, and everyone faces it differently. However, my mom knew that good food and company were the most precious gifts in times of mourning. Sure, it's expected that friends and families bring over meals that can be quickly cooked and cleaned up in times of distress, but that wasn't enough for my parents. It was their mission to provide the most personal and intimate experiences for their customers and their community. It was a daily spectacle with multiple matinees and prime time slots.

When I got home from school each day, I would run up the stairs to our apartment and get ready for work. Yes, work. We would host every family having a wake with us that day in our apartment for a meal. It didn't matter whether there was one funeral or ten. Every family member and friend of the deceased was invited.

It was a multi-day setup as well. We would have ordered the food from the grocery store across the street the day before and after school, before heading home, I would stop at the grocery store and pick it up. Most of the time, I could barely carry it myself and even had to make several trips on busier days.

We would set up stations around the kitchen where the families could build their sandwiches. My job began with rolling the meats like roast beef, turkey, and ham and layering them in a circle on the tray. Next, I would dump a container of coleslaw in a large bowl, and the same with the potato salad. A long silver serving tray would host all kinds of pickles, any pickle you could think of for their sandwiches. I would then open the many loaves of white and wheat bread and display them around circle trays, making it all look as

44

neat as possible. I would then turn on the 60 cup coffee maker, throw Pepsi, 7-Up, and beer in coolers. Next came the tablecloths. I would lay them out across the long table in our dining room that could seat 20 people at a time. If we needed more space, I would have to be ready to set up several extra folding card tables and chairs throughout the apartment. I would place paper plates, napkins, plastic forks, and knives at each place setting, along with a styrofoam cup. We would have ketchup, mustard, mayo, salt, and pepper, along with sugar and cream dispersed down the middle of the table. After that, our Family Food Service was open for business!

My mom or I would call down to the manager on duty and say, "Send up the first family!"

They would then make a quick announcement to inform the first family, who would come upstairs rather quickly. Aside from being hungry, most people were also interested to see what an apartment above a funeral home looked like.

Each family would file into our apartment and find a seat. They would grab their plates, make their sandwiches, choose their sides, grab a drink, and head back to their spot. My family and I would be ready to clean up any garbage or refill any food or drink items needed.

Once the first family finished, we would quickly clean the space, refresh the food platters, and ask the second family to make their way upstairs. Most of the time, it wasn't just the immediate family but also their extended family and close friends. My parents wanted to extend this comfort to those who were grieving, and, as a result, we could feed over 100 people in a single night.

Aside from being present for food service and cleaning duty, on special occasions, such as Tuesdays or Fridays, or any day ending with "y," my mom would also require that I perform to lift their spirits. While she thought it was cute, I thought it was horrifying. Reflecting on those moments and trying to understand their perspectives, seeing a child scream a cheer or poorly play the piano, accompanied by an Irish jig, was probably the last thing these grieving families wanted to experience. I would also wear costumes from plays I would in and perform my lines (without any other characters to make sense of the scene) or model a dress for an upcoming school dance. I hated every minute of it so much that it impacted how I felt about trying new extracurricular activities. When I was thinking about trying out for the volleyball team, I decided that there was no way my mom would let me play volleyball in the house with a bunch of customers around and the possibility of breaking something or hitting someone. So, I gave it a shot. When I eventually got on the volleyball team, my mom started making me show off my uniform to the families and play the game without a ball. It was traumatizing.

Finally, when we were done serving all the families dinner, I would begin the role of the clean-up crew. I would fold up the chairs and tables and bring them downstairs to be set up and stored in the viewing rooms. Wakes were so big back then we needed hundreds of chairs everywhere. A wake was a social outing as much as it was a moment of closure and respect for the dead. People lingered in the viewing rooms, the lobby, the hallways, and even the large community room in the basement and talked with each other for hours. After years of carrying these chairs, I became a pro and was able to bring down four at a time, two under each arm. I would walk down the stairs and through a big wooden doorframe, separating our apartment and the funeral home. I would start by lining them up in each viewing room until there were no more chairs in the apartment. I would then quickly empty the ashtrays, make more coffee for the people still sitting and chatting, and then I was allowed to go back to my life.

But it helped form who I am today, a grown woman, taking care of kids and dogs, participating on boards and engaging with clubs, maintaining friendships, and serving dinners daily. Not much has changed, but I am happy.

After the dinners would finish for the night, a few hours after school ended, it would be time to begin my homework and eat dinner myself. And yes, I would have the same sandwiches, potato salad, and coleslaw. Then our Great Dane, Smokey, and I would jump into my twin bed and go to sleep before getting ready to do it all again the next day.

It's kind of funny thinking back on how much those experiences have shaped who I am today. I don't have a traditional approach to death. Of course, I mourn, and I grieve, but most of all, I am ready for a party. This is probably because I was trained to perform and execute under emotional pressure. I'm thankful that I was able to thrive in that environment.

Some of my friends, on the other hand, felt differently about this experience. It was always an exciting opportunity to observe my friends in a new way when they would stay over. Some of them found these experiences fun and wanted to come over and help at these dinners more often, and others found it crazy and never wanted to step foot back into our family's apartment. There were a lot of rumors and assumptions about what our house looked like. They believed our house must have smelled like flowers at all times or that we would live in rooms with dimmed lighting. These thoughts always made me laugh because living above a funeral home felt normal to me as my friend's houses did.

I'll never forget the first time I had a friend's sleepover. I was ten years old, and I was in sixth grade. My friend, Julie, had agreed to stay over at my house one weekend, not knowing what she was getting into.

Julie was the same age as me, and we went to school together. We had been friends for a while, and I was excited to have her over. I had never had a friend stay over at my apartment before, and this was Julie's first time visiting EVER! Talk about a unique introduction!

She asked me how to get to my apartment, and this is where the hilarity begins.

There was a back door on the left side of the building, and it was dedicated solely to the two apartments upstairs. My family and I lived in one apartment, and my grandfather lived in the other.

Just to paint a quick picture for you, my grandfather was a classy man. He was always wearing a red velvet smoking jacket, with his black dress pants and slippers, holding a dirty gin martini with a bottle of Pepto Bismol stuffed in one jacket pocket and Listerine in the other. He was very sophisticated, and he was my best friend growing up. Quite the character, if I do say so myself. He was a gentleman's gentleman.

So, you can imagine the look on Julie's face when she knocked on the wrong door.

My grandfather answered, giggling and surprised, "Hello there, young lady! How can I help you?"

Julie shyly responded, "I'm here for the sleepover. . . "

Grandfather replied humorously, "Well, you're welcome to stay here, but I think you'll have much more fun next door with Sheila!"

She giggled and knocked on the other door. My grandfather waited with her as I darted to the door to let Julie in. He escorted Julie into the apartment and wished us a fun evening. Together, Julie and I bounced back to my bedroom, ready for all of the shenanigans to begin!

What I didn't know was that Julie's dad teased her before she came over. He joked about all of the scary things that would probably happen during her visit, from ghost sightings to dead bodies rising from the caskets. She was petrified when she got to the front door.

As we were running to my room, she was greeted by Smokey, our larger-than-life Great Dane. Meeting a dog that was the same height as her, might I add, put her over the edge! She was shaking in fear and suggested that she go home and come back another time.

I told her there were a lot of fun things that we could do. Understandably, she questioned me.

"What can we do here that's fun? We're in a funeral home."

"Let's bring Smokey downstairs and let him loose in the funeral home! I bet it will surprise everyone!"

She reluctantly agreed, thinking that it would be humorous to see this massive dog interrupt the events happening on the first floor.

The first time I let Smokey out downstairs, it was an accident. The reactions from the crowds of people made me laugh so uncontrollably that I saved this experience for special moments when I needed a laugh or times when my friends, like Julie, were scared.

That night was the perfect setting for Smokey's show. There were at least 100 people in the funeral home for wakes. I was giggling as we brought him downstairs, and Julie began to ease a little. She could see how happy and excited I was about this and started feeling the same way.

We got to the bottom of the stairs and counted to three before opening the large wooden door to let Smokey loose!

"One... Two... Three!"

The door flung open, and Smokey ran like a racehorse through the funeral home! There were no areas off-limits when he was downstairs, as he was rarely allowed on that floor. Imagine being at a wake, and a pony-sized dog starts jumping through the crowds, knocking over flower stands, and even licking the corpses! It was an incredible sight while it lasted. We quickly lost sight of Smokey because of his speed. We were able to find him again because of the guests screaming in other rooms.

"THERE'S A DOG IN HERE!"

Smokey was a hit. Maybe not with the crowds, but for Julie and me!

I had forgotten to bring a leash with us, so it was challenging to try and get him back upstairs. Julie and I were in sweatpants, t-shirts, and slippers, which was not ideal for chasing a gazelle-like canine. There was almost no hope of controlling this animal.

After running through the whole building, down to the basement, and chasing him through the community room, embalming room, casket room, and more, we finally coaxed him into the elevator. We quickly shut the big folding door and then tried to help Smokey calm down. He was so excited about his run that he was acting wild!

Julie muttered, "I hope we can take this all the way upstairs!"

"We can't. . . We have to walk Smokey through the crowd again."

We arrived on the first floor, and I was nervous Smokey would get loose again. As the door opened, I saw my dad, absolutely furious, on the other side.

"Sheila, what is going on here?!"

He opened the folding door, took Smokey by the collar, and gracefully led him straight upstairs through the crowds as Julie and I followed.

The people began parting as they saw my dad and Smokey walking through. It was like the parting of the Red Sea, and everyone moved out of the way to let a man and his colossal dog walk by.

"How did this happen?" My dad asked frustratingly. "There are two door in between here and downstairs!"

As we silently shrugged, my dad sighed and responded, "Just don't do it again," and then walked back downstairs.

The second the door shut, Julie and I burst out laughing! We were crying from laughing so hard.

We had worked up an appetite from all of the running and decided to grab some food. We had the classic sandwich and potato salad mix leftover from the families that were over for dinner earlier.

Julie was surprised we had so much food available, and she didn't even know half of it.

"I wish my family ate like this all the time!" Julie exclaimed.

I giggled along while thinking to myself, "I doubt that!"

It was late at night, and the funerals were beginning to end for the evening. We decided to get into bed before my dad came back upstairs. Smokey and I were in my bed, and Julie was in a sleeping bag on the floor. Smokey had no manners and eventually moved to the floor and laid across Julie. Smokey shed a lot, and Julie kept getting so much fur in her mouth that she couldn't sleep, so we sat up and talked.

I told her more about living above the funeral home. I didn't realize it right away, but I terrorized her by telling her that my bed was a few floors directly above the embalming room, and there were probably dead people lying in that room now.

She leaped from the bed to the wall and turned on the light, shouting, "I will never be able to sleep here! Let's play a game; otherwise, I have to go home."

We stayed up playing games all night and had a blast. She stayed over almost every weekend after that.

We are friends for life! Actually, we're friends for afterlife!

# CHAPTER 5

---

# The Mafia Made Me Do It

The thing about living above a funeral home is that we never stop working.

Even when we are closed. There's no time off for death. Everyone dies. And once they die, their bodies have to be properly taken care of, remembered, respected, and then buried or cremated. These people who die can be from anywhere, believing in whatever religion they want, valuing whichever culture they choose, with their own traditions, including the Mafia. The old-time Mafia I'm talking about lives by rules, regulations. Their lives and culture are based on respect and family.

Also, they generally don't want to call attention to themselves and their families and prefer to live under the radar as much as possible. Because of this, any Mafia man we buried had his wake at night. They would start promptly at midnight and by 6:00AM, there was no sign they were ever there.

I remember the first time I directed a Mafia wake alone.

I was in high school, and my parents were out of town. I had no idea how the night was going to go so, naturally, I was a bit nervous. I mean, it was going to be a building filled with the Mafia, and me. I had to keep reminding myself that the Mafia men are respectful and responsible, especially in situations like this, so I wouldn't be concerned about what shenanigans might happen throughout the evening. At about 10 PM, I received a phone call.

"Sheila?"

Not knowing who was on the other line, I hesitatingly responded "Yes?"

"This is Anthony."

"Hello, Anthony. How can I help you?"

"I want to go over how tonight's wake is going to go."

OH! A Mafia guy! I wondered to myself how he could have known my name already, but that thought quickly passed as he began going over his expectations for the evening.

"OK, I'm listening."

"We will arrive at about 11:45 pm with his family. From that point on, we will hold the wake, and it all ends at 7 AM. We just need you to make sure everything is set up correctly, the coffee is made, and to ensure that we have enough prayer cards and condolence books laid out. We will take it all from there. Please meet me at 11:30 PM to go over everything again."

"Yes, I'll be ready."

I wasn't aware that this was the usual setup for Mafia funerals. But it seemed as if I really didn't have much to do. I thought I would stay in the office with the lights off for a little while just to ensure that everything was going well before leaving them to mourn their loved one.

I then went downstairs to the basement to check in with the embalmers. They had the body dressed and ready to go in the bronze casket they had made. They always chose the most expensive caskets that money could buy.

I then went back upstairs to set up the wake room, or chapel as we called it. A few minutes later we had the casket in place, and then we had to bring in the flowers. We carried in hundreds of flower arrangements that were delivered earlier in the day and put out hundreds of prayer cards. I set up five condolence books for people to sign, made sure we had double the amount of ashtrays out, brewed up three of the sixty-cup coffee pots, and everything was ready to go. I ran upstairs to the apartment to get myself ready with about fifteen minutes left to spare before Anthony would arrive.

Working in this industry you learned how to pull yourself together quickly. Choosing our outfits was easy because our uniform was to wear all black. My closet had one shade throughout it, and I could pick up any skirt, shirt, pants, or jacket I wanted and it would always look professional and respectful. It took me years to get out of the black-wearing habit, but I have to say I still keep about half my closet filled with all black.

Ten minutes later I was downstairs and ready to welcome Anthony. 11:30 PM came and, sure enough, a black car pulled into the parking lot on the dot. The driver walked around, opened the back car door, and out came one of the scariest, biggest, most Italian-looking men I have ever seen. He opened his mouth to introduce himself and out came a deep voice, it seemed much deeper in person.

"Hello Sheila, I'm Anthony."

"Hello, Anthony, good to meet you. Let's go inside."

Anthony looked around, inspecting the Funeral home. I showed him the way to the chapel. We had put the deceased in our largest chapel, knowing there would be a lot of people. Anthony inspected the body, brushed off his lapel, turned around, and took a long hard look at the room, the flowers.

"Okay. Take me to the coffee room."

As I walked with him, more cars were beginning to pull up. Large Italian men were coming in with food, alcohol, ice buckets, tables, and more. They turned the Funeral home into their personal bar and restaurant.

Anthony then said, "We are all set but, Sheila, I must warn you. Tonight is going to be very busy. There are going to be tons of people coming. I have directed several strong men to keep watch in the parking lot, four more on the front door, and two others on the back door, just as a precaution. You know how these things can get."

I didn't really know how these things could get, as I had never participated in one before, but I did know that Mafia wakes were respectful, responsible, and sometimes targeted. I felt uneasy not being able to stay downstairs the whole time but I also felt somewhat comfortable and safe. If anyone could protect me, I was sure it was these big Italian guys!

I think Anthony could tell I was experiencing these emotions because he looked at me and said: "Don't you worry about anything, Sheila. We will take care of everything."

And just like that, the wake began. Car, after car, after car started pulling up. The first three cars that pulled up were the immediate family. Anthony greeted them one by one with kisses on both sides of their faces and took them into the chapel. The majority of the other cars were Mafia men in dark suits, all looking like they just walked off the movie set for *The Godfather*. They were shaking hands with each other, talking, drinking coffee, whiskey, smoking, walking around. Some were seated in huddles talking, but they just kept coming.

I watched a lot of it from my upstairs apartment. It was like an Italian parade of nice, black cars with big Italian men. The funny thing I noticed was that no one was leaving; they all came and stayed. I decided to go down and get a closer look. So I sat in the office, looking through the big window we had looking out the front door, and took it all in.

The funeral home phone rang at 1:30 AM and I picked it up.

"Hello, this is Sheila, how may I help you?"

"Hey Sheila, how's it going?" It was my dad calling to check in. Even when he was on vacation, he was never really away.

"Fine, but very interesting. There are many people here, and no one is leaving. They set up tons of food, alcohol, and people are pouring in."

My dad laughed and said "Yeah that's normal for the Mafia. It's all okay. Nothing will happen, and they will clean it all up after. I'm not worried, and you shouldn't be either."

"OK, thanks for calling Dad. Talk to you tomorrow."

As the night went on, they brought in more food, more booze and more people. I thought I was on a movie set waiting for someone to say, "Cut that's a wrap" or something along those lines. I couldn't believe that this huge group of people were all together, and there was no chaos or trouble.

Around three o'clock in the morning, a big limo pulled up. A lot of the men walked over to the windows, watching to see this person get out of the car. His driver opened the car door, and out stepped a huge man. Bigger than all of the other men I had already seen. He put his cigarette out on the ground, and men began running up to help him. They were opening the door, straightening their ties, clearing their throats, and forming lines to shake his hand as he walked into the Funeral home.

I thought, wow, this must be the head man, the big guy, the Godfather. I remember thinking how cool this all was. To watch these interactions and traditions first hand, and experience all I imagined might happen, was extraordinary to me.

The night was continuing on, and it seemed as if it would never end. I couldn't imagine that they would be able to clean all of this up and be gone by seven, with this many people here. At four in the morning, Anthony noticed I was in the office, practically falling asleep.

He came into the room and quietly said "Sheila, if you can make some more coffee, put out more prayer cards, and retire for the night, I'll make sure everything is cleaned up, taken out, and done for the funeral tomorrow."

"Okay, thank you. I'm tired, and I will be working in the morning for the funeral before school, but I can make sure that all gets done." After getting those few things sorted, I went upstairs to our apartment, looked out my bedroom window into the parking lot, and saw a sea of men in dark suits. Some were smoking cigarettes and cigars, they were all walking around and talking. I took a glance into the parking lot and noticed all of the Cadillacs, Limos, Lincoln Continentals. Their drivers were standing around their cars, their faces looked as if they were keeping an eye out for anything suspicious. I had never felt more protected in my whole life.

I changed into my pajamas and got in bed. My alarm went off at six o'clock to get ready for the next funeral. I prayed that there wouldn't be a mess for me to rapidly clean up, but had a faint bit of faith in Anthony's words.

I showered, and I got in my school uniform. I went downstairs, still a little hesitant, remembering the number of ashtrays, the hundreds of coffee cups and plastic cups, all the food leftovers, not to mention the carpets, and thought the bathroom lights probably hadn't been turned off. By the time I got down the stairs, I had worked myself up so much that I was completely filled with worry. I was an absolute basket case anticipating the amount of trouble I was about to be in.

I closed my eyes as I approached the funeral home door down the stairs from my apartment and braced the door handle not knowing what to expect. I slowly pulled open the door and I smelled the air around me to help prepare what I was about to see. Assuming it would smell of smoke, pasta, and alcohol, I was shocked and completely relieved to smell a clean, fresh, scent.

I slowly opened my eyes. I walked into the lobby with my jaw dropped. The whole space had been beautifully sanitized. I took a few more steps and looked around in complete awe. Everything was just as Anthony had said it would be at 7:00 AM, and everything was good. Better than good! The ashtrays were emptied, the bathrooms cleaned, the carpets vacuumed, I ran to the coffee room, and the pots were off and cleaned. I ran to the chapel, and the seats were all organized, and the body was gone. The tables and chairs had been removed, and the liquor bottles and food had been taken away. You would never know just a short time before this moment that this place had been filled with hundreds of people.

Just then, there was a knock on the front door. I pulled my key out from my pocket and as I was opening the door with the key, I said out loud to myself, how did this get locked?

Anthony heard me say this and as I opened the door he handed me a key and calmly said, "Sheila, I told you I would take care of everything, didn't I?"

"You sure did, Anthony. Thank you."

"Now, as far as last night goes, we won't talk about it. Today is the funeral and there will be different people. We will leave last night as it is, in the past."

"Okay, Anthony, no problem." And with that, I shut the door.

Everything was ready for the funeral, and I didn't have to do much of anything. What a way to get the day started!

I went into the office and began asking around who could drop me off at school. Out of my peripheral vision, I could see that there were eleven flower cars lining up that would take all the flowers to the church and cemetery. The hearse and 20 limos were lined up. People were pouring into the parking lot to be lined up for the procession, and Anthony was right. I didn't recognize anyone from the night before.

For the funeral, there were women, kids and families. There were still lovely cars but now also vans, smaller cars, and family cars. It was going to be a big funeral but, yes, a completely different day than the night before.

Johnny, one of the funeral home's drivers, caught me in the middle of my flurry of questions running through my mind and said he could run me to school. As we walked out into the parking lot, I quickly looked around, and I saw Anthony. He tipped his hat to me and gave me a gun trigger hand signal saying I did a good job.

I smiled and nodded my head to him as well. I thought to myself, *Wow, what a night!* I couldn't imagine how I could have a typical day at school after all of this!

Another day with the living, another night with the dead, and all of it with the Mafia.

This was my life.

# CHAPTER 6

—

# After School Snacks and Heart Attacks

Living in a penthouse sounds much more luxurious than living on the top floor of a funeral home, doesn't it? Yes, the penthouse sounds like paradise.

However, I knew the truth. And it was nothing like the Garden of Eden, I will tell you that much!

Living above a funeral home never gave us any free time. It really was a Twenty-four-hour a day, 365-day-a-year gig. It's no secret, people die all the time. There's no closing time for death. Even if the funeral home is closed for the night, and the services have ended, and all of the employees have gone home, dead bodies were still dropped off, all night long. And not just one or two, but sometimes ten or twelve. If there were a lot of them, the embalmers would have to stay all night to prepare the bodies. This made for a stressful working and living environment. You never knew how busy a day could become, or how emotionally drained you could end up feeling. I used to say that our family ate, drank, and breathed death. We could never get away from it.

And if I felt stressed out, my parents felt it tenfold. This was their life. I at least got to go to school, participate in activities, visit friends' homes, and more before coming back to it. But they lived above the funeral home and worked in it every day. My dad would wake up, shower, and go directly downstairs. While our funeral home had 12 visiting rooms, sometimes we could have eleven funerals in one day.

You see, once someone dies, whether at home, at a hospital, or out and about, you call a funeral home. They in turn have the body picked up and brought back for embalming. Some religions or direct burials didn't need or didn't allow embalming, but if the family of the deceased was going to have a wake, meaning family and friends would come to our building to pay their respects to the deceased, the body was then embalmed. This process of embalming preserved the body so the public could respectively see their friend and loved one in the manner they were used to seeing them alive.

Wakes also varied in a few ways. They could be hours, a day, or last several days and the funeral service was usually the day following the wake.

While the wake itself may sound like a big undertaking, the funerals required a lot more logistical planning. The funeral day started at the funeral home. This was typically another private moment for the immediate family with prayers depending on the religion. They would have their last "pass by," which is when everyone walks past the casket to see the person one more time and say goodbye, followed by the ceremonial closing of the casket. Chosen friends or family members would be given white gloves and were known as "Pallbearers," and they would assist in carrying the casket throughout the funeral day. The white gloves were used to show respect to the deceased. The Pallbearers would help transport the casket to the hearse and the funeral day would continue. If there weren't any pallbearers chosen before the service, our employees would serve in that role.

The hearses would arrive in the attached garage of the funeral home and there would be one hearse ready to receive the casket. They would then perform the ceremonial lifting of the casket and place it in the hearse. Once the casket was safely in the hearse, it would pull out of the garage and begin the processional. The garage was a drive-through building leading to the street, which made the processions more efficient. As the hearse was pulling out of the garage, the cars would begin to line up, or the family could have arranged for limousines to transport the family members to follow their loved ones to the church or the cemetery. If limousines were arranged, our drivers would pick up the family members at one home and be with them all day.

The funeral procession could go a few ways once it left the funeral home. The families would either choose to first go to a place of worship, then another funeral procession to a cemetery for more closing prayers or remarks, or simply straight to the cemetery. While hundreds and sometimes thousands of people would attend wakes, this was also sometimes expected for the funerals and processions could be miles long!

On particularly busier days with several funerals planned, we could have upwards of ten people hired just to maintain traffic in the parking lot. It would sometimes become a maze of cars, hearses, and limousines, and it was crucial that we kept the families together and didn't direct them to the wrong processional! We would try to stagger the starting times because hundreds of cars would come in the morning. Keeping all this straight, without the technology of any kind mind you, was chaotic, to say the least.

The traffic directors would ask each car which funeral they were attending. The visitors would tell the directors the name, and they would be directed to the line of cars ready for the procession later in the day. They were also given stickers for the front and back of their car, which were orange and said "Funeral" in big black bold font so they could be in the funeral procession and go through stop lights and intersections legally without being separated from the group.

The few of us who were left at the funeral home after the procession had left would run around like chickens without heads to get ready for the next wakes to start.

We had a full-time cleaning crew who would begin cleaning the chapels, bathrooms, coffee rooms, and so on to prepare for more visitors, which helped us tremendously because preparing for a wake or a funeral in the middle of the day is not a walk in the park. It's more of like a run through a blizzard across a lake while being chased by the shattering ice behind us. We were always gearing for the next event while being followed by the aftermath of the events prior.

The embalmers would start their preparations the night before. Each evening before leaving for the night, they would review their schedule to ensure the correct bodies were fully prepared in their caskets for the next morning so that the wakes could begin efficiently and on time regardless of whether it was planned for first thing in the morning, the afternoon or the evening.

When the next wake was going to begin, the funeral director would go down the embalming room, retrieve the casket, and take the elevator back up to the main floor. Even if there were several wakes beginning around the same time, they would have to be taken up one at a time. The casket would then be rolled to its dedicated chapel and the rest of the preparations would begin.

We would change the display boards in the lobby to help visitors know where to go and the time of the wake. There's nothing more heartbreaking than to have to escort mourning loved ones from a chapel because they didn't take note of the time frame. Those boards would also include information about funerals if needed. As visitors would look for the chapel, there would also be a display board above the doorway at the dedicated chapel. Sometimes it would get confusing when a few people with the same last name were being waked but had no relation. These display boards helped keep everyone organized.

Aside from the display boards, we would also have to change the flowers, the prayer cards, grab a new sign-in book and add any other personalized requests such as poster boards or videos playing in the background.

All of this had to be done at least 15 minutes prior to the family arriving. So there was always something for everyone to do!

We wanted the experience to feel seamless to them, and to give them an immediate opportunity to have a peaceful encounter with their loved one, and they would usually arrive at least 10 minutes early each time.

While there was always hesitation for this moment, families also felt pulled to this experience to find closure. It's part of the healing process for the living.

When the deceased's immediate family arrived first, we would guide them to their chapel and then leave them alone for about 15 minutes to have some privacy. It's one thing to talk about your loved one's death, and it's another one to see them motionless in a casket. It hits differently, and we knew that even though our presence wouldn't change their experience, we felt it was more intimate to just be them together. After that short time, we would remind the families of the locations of the bathrooms, the coffee rooms, and anywhere else they may need to remember to go throughout their time with us. Then we would ask if anyone needed anything additional.

This was when the flood gates would open. You'd think they would request a bottle of water maybe, but boy oh boy, that was the farthest thought from their mind. They would usually ask us to change things about their loved one's body.

"Can you cut their hair? Or maybe curl it more? It looks too long, or maybe too straight."

"Is there time to change his shirt?"

"Can we paint her nails?"

"Do you still have their glasses? They only wore them when they were reading, but they might make her look more like herself."

"Why does their face look bloated? Can we push their cheeks back?"

"Do their hands have to be clasped?"

These requests were usually overwhelming for our embalmers at such a pivotal moment, with no time to spare, so we would try to help as much as we could but also took into account that these people were grieving.

Sometimes families would say, "Everything looks great. You've done a wonderful job of honoring our loved one," and we would breathe a huge sigh of relief. We would then leave them be, and remind them that one of us was always available to help in any way and assure them that we would be around to help make sure their day went smoothly.

Funeral Directors are present to do just that, direct the funeral. It's almost as if we were the conductors of a large symphony without knowing what instruments were present. Our stress level never lowered and the anticipation of what could go wrong never left us. And believe me, things did go wrong.

We get it, death is an emotional experience, and in some cases, extremely emotional. These extreme emotions would sometimes cause incredibly dramatic events to take place.

Some family members would get completely inebriated, and their emotions would usually lead them in one of two ways. They would either become enveloped by their sadness and sob louder than a whole room of mourners combined, or they would scream and yell at anyone and everyone.

Other times, mourners would behave dramatically, and those individuals would throw themselves across the casket and perform heartbreaking monologues for the room to witness.

A few times, we even caught a few swindlers trying to steal jewelry or mementos from the deceased. Rings or earrings were usually the targets. "Mom always wanted me to have this ring! I need to take it now before it's too late!"

Most of the time, our biggest concerns were family quarrels. People from all different walks of life present themselves at a wake to pay their respects and to gain closure. Sometimes, those walks have led certain family members or friends on diverging paths, and when those paths would cross again at a wake, where emotions are heightened already, it would create the perfect storm.

So I think it's safe to agree that while these are traumatic experiences for those who have lost loved ones, the directors were always trying to stay on track. It's a special kind of stress because as a funeral director you know you are helping families through some of their most challenging moments, but you are also holding yourself to professional standards without really any control over the situation.

This kind of stress builds up over time, and for my parents, it would build up quickly. They decided no matter what, they needed to get away, for any amount of time, several times a year, at any cost. They would go on whirlwind trips all over the world for 6-8 weeks at a time. During those times they would hire different babysitters. Sometimes it would be an aunt or uncle, other times family friends. We would also stay at people's homes and every time it was someone different. One week it could be a married couple, the next with a family of six, or we were farmed out to our friend's homes. But my parents made it a priority to go away a few times a year.

I'll never forget their vacation when I was 14. I was the only one home and my mom asked our cleaning lady, Mrs. Lincoln, to watch me. I remember her ashy skin with brown and grey hair, which she always wore in a bun and usually had a dishtowel tied to her apron prepared for any spill or mess at any time. She was probably in her late 60s, a quiet but larger lady, and I remember that we got along well. Mrs. Lincoln agreed to stay and she moved into our apartment above the funeral home. My parents were expected to be gone for seven weeks this time, and she was ready to be with me the whole time.

I was relieved because that meant I didn't have to move around each week! I was happy to be there with Mrs. Lincoln and knew that this time would fly by.

Mrs. Lincoln continued her cleaning jobs and took on some extra cooking for dinners. My mom had filled the fridge and the two freezers we had with everything we might need for those seven weeks. Chicken, burgers, TV dinners, fish sticks, tater tots, and more. Ms. Lincoln would try to help me with my homework sometimes, but would usually send me downstairs to speak with the managers for assistance.

She also took on Smokey, our Great Dane! I would let him out in the morning before school, but during the day she would try to walk him around the block. "Try" being key word. He was a force of nature. I don't know who had it harder during those walks, Mrs. Lincoln, or Smokey!

For the first two weeks, everything was great. I would wake up and Mrs. Lincoln would have breakfast waiting for me. As I ate, she would feed Smokey. I would let him out, then get ready for school. Once I was dressed and ready to go I would head to school.

But I remember a few days after those two weeks there was one morning that felt differently. Mrs. Lincoln wasn't as chipper when I woke up and I thought she might be getting sick. I let Smokey out and got ready as normal and went to school. That afternoon I came straight home from school and I heard the vacuum cleaner going which wasn't unusual. Mrs. Lincoln was always cleaning something. Always the perfectionist!

However, this time I walked into the living room to see how she was doing and I saw Mrs. Lincoln slumped over the vacuum. I thought to myself she must be checking something on the vacuum.

"Hi Mrs. Lincoln, how are you?" I asked curiously.

Silence.

She did not budge. She did not make a noise. She did not do anything.

Thinking maybe she couldn't hear me over the vacuum I repeated myself louder, "Hi Mrs. Lincoln, I'm home, how are you?"

Silence.

I walked closer to her and she looked terrible. She looked sick.

She looked dead.

Now, even though I had been around hundreds of dead bodies at this point, I still didn't know what to do about Mrs. Lincoln.

I quickly called downstairs and ask the manager on duty to come up immediately.

As I was shaking, I managed to blurt out "I think there is something terribly wrong with Mrs. Lincoln, she's not moving, she's not talking."

We hung up and I ran to the door.

The manager came running up the stairs and I was waiting for him.

He hurried to the living room and when he saw her he stopped in his tracks. He slowly made his way towards her and observed her as I did. Then he touched her arm and she slammed to the ground. He kneeled and put his head next to her mouth to hear if she was breathing.

I turned off the vacuum to quiet the room.

He then sat up and held her wrist. He was feeling for a pulse. After a few moments, he laid her wrist back down and quietly said, "She's dead."

She had a heart attack while vacuuming and her apron got caught in the top of the vacuum and that's what balanced her over the vacuum.

He called the coroner who came straight over. He determined that she had not been dead long and that the heart attack killed her instantly.

I was in shock.

This was terrible. She had been so nice to me.

I went to a friend's house for the next two days so that Mrs. Lincoln could be taken to the embalming room and the apartment could be cleaned.

I went to her wake and funeral a few days later. At the wake, her daughter approached me. "Sheila, are your parents going to be coming home soon?"

"I think they said a few more weeks."

"Okay, can I call you after the funeral? We will arrange a schedule to take care of you. We don't want you home alone for a few weeks!"

"Okay" I said.

A few hours later I was back in the apartment and I sat next to the phone, waiting for her call.

It never came.

I wasn't sure what to do. I didn't have anywhere to stay, and my parents were still away. I certainly had enough food, so I decided "I can do this myself!"

The next morning I got myself up, made food, fed and took out Smokey, and went to school.

The funeral home was busier than ever, so no one noticed the fact that I was alone or had time to think about how I was doing.

The embalmers would call every evening around midnight to let me know they were leaving for the night.

Being 14 years old and alone in a funeral home at night was terrifying. I was completely petrified. Unbeknownst to me, being alone meant that I also had to let the dead bodies in and bring them to the embalming room all night long, which Ms. Lincoln had been responsible for up till now. Each time the phone rang I became paralyzed with fear.

One night the phone rang and the operator said, "This is the international operator, I have a collect call from China and a Matt Lamb on the line, will you accept the charges?"

"Yes," I said.

My dad yelled, "Hello Sheila, how are you?"

"I'm fine, Dad," I said. There was about a three-second delay each way.

"How is everything going, what's new, anything?"

"Well, Mrs. Lincoln died and I've been alone."

"What?"

"I'm letting the dead bodies in at night and getting myself to and from school, and taking care of Smokey."

"Ok, good. Ok, good. We'll be home in a few weeks. Love you!" And that was about it.

"Love you too, Dad."

We hung up the phone.

Later in life, I learned that after that phone call my mom asked how everything was going at home and my dad said "Just fine."

Ha!

After that call, I assumed this would be my future for the next few weeks. I decided to take some food out of the freezer and defrost it to cook it. But I didn't know how to plan for defrosting food and ended up spoiling most of it as I left it out for a few days. I ended up having to throw most of it away.

However, I made it through those last few weeks on my own! Smokey was fine, the dead bodies were all transported properly, and no one noticed that I was alone.

My parents came home after three more weeks away and I told my mom all that happened. "Matt!" My mom yelled, "Why didn't you tell me this when you called Sheila a few weeks ago?" She was furious.

He simply said, "you would have wanted to come home, and I could tell that she was fine. She was taking care of herself and the business, and we needed the rest. See, it all worked out fine."

My mom was enraged. She stormed away from the living room to begin unpacking but first went to the freezer to take out some food to defrost for dinner.

She looked into the freezer and saw that most of the food was gone.

"Oh, Sheila, I'm so glad you ate well! I'm happy that there was enough food for you to keep your nourishment up and I'm so proud of you for teaching yourself to cook it! This makes me feel better."

It took everything in my power to not start laughing out loud. I figured she didn't need to know what really happened to the frozen food so I just smiled and nodded.

I just figured I'd wait until they got the bill for the house account from the restaurant across the street! Cha-ching! Thanks for the chicken rings!

# CHAPTER 7

---

# Prom Date Disaster

While I was living alone above the funeral home, I was often asked who cooked for me. It wasn't common during that time to not have a home cooked meal on a regular basis, let alone live above a funeral home alone during teenage years.

I didn't suffer, though. I was well taken care of by another family - the mob.

Every day after school and extracurricular activities, I would stop by a local restaurant and supper club in the south side of Chicago. It was a stone's throw away from the funeral home. Literally, I could walk to the end of the parking lot and across the street and be greeted by their bright, bold sign.

They served anything and everything you could think of! You name it, they would make it. I actually got lucky in that sense because I always got to eat exactly what I wanted!

They also had an entertainment room where they had live shows and entertainers. Our family loved this place so much that we hosted 90% of our luncheons here. We knew they could hold a lot of people and their food was good. What more could we ask for?

After going there for years I got to know the owners and everyone in their tight circle very well. Even before my parents moved away we ate here often, and ordered out even more often! Sometimes I would even make it there for breakfast before school. This restaurant was part of the family. And I loved it.

Every time I walked in I noticed the table near the back corner of the dining space. I would wave to them and they would nod back. It always seemed as if the same people were there, in the same seats, every day. Almost as if they never left! I eventually figured out their names. The guy on furthest end was called "Boss" and he had the best view of the restaurant. He would see everyone who walked in and out of the building. On either side of him was Anthony and Rocky. At the other end of the table was "Three Fingers." I never figured out how he got his nickname, but I am sure your imagination can help you out there, and Guido was always running around the table keeping busy. Sometimes Boss would wave me over and they'd ask about my life.

"Sheila, how is school going? Did you make the volleyball team again? How's that school play? Do you need anything? You're not still dating that non-Italian boy, are you? You know the Italian men are the best!"

We all had a really good friendship. Over the years I would sit and chat with them often, and sometimes even ask for advice about life or work.

When I was 17 and my parents were out of the house, my friends and I would pop over and ask if there were any extra seats for the show. They always had room for us and treated us like royalty. We would be served Italian feasts with all of the wine and beer we could imagine. It was the best way to spend a Friday night with my friends.

Whenever we would leave the owners would ask us if we needed help getting home safely, and even though we were always headed to the funeral home across the street and didn't need help, they watched from the windows to make sure. They really took care of us, and I loved it.

However, there were a few times I wasn't too keen on how much they cared.

I remember one day Anthony joined me at the bar as I was eating dinner a few nights before a school dance. After chatting a little bit about normal stuff, Anthony inquired about my upcoming plans.

"Sheila, it's almost prom night, isn't it?"

"It sure is!"

He leaned in closer with a half smile and asked, "Who is taking you? A nice Italian boy I hope!"

I giggled and said, "Oh, my friend Collin and I are going together."

He leaned back a little bit with one eyebrow lifted. "Collin doesn't sound Italian."

"Nope, he's Irish!"

"Alright, well just to be safe, why don't you bring Collin over for a drink before you head to the dance. We just want to see you all dressed up before the big night."

"Okay, we'll see you at 7."

It wasn't out of the norm for Anthony to chat with me, and invite me over before big school events. They always supported me as if I was their own family and cheered me on as I continued to learn and grow. However, they never asked to meet a boy I was with before. It was an interesting request but I didn't see any harm in it. I was throwing a pre-party at my apartment so I figured we would just pop over for a few minutes before heading to the dance.

Shortly later, it was prom night. The party was roaring! The usual suspects were there including my best friends Julie, Grace, Elaine, Rosie, and Meg, along with 50 of my closest classmates. It was so much fun that I almost forgot Collin and I had to run across the street to meet with the boys.

"Collin! We need to run across the restaurant real quick before the dance, the guys want to meet you!"

He nervously responded, "Okay?"

We got there and Anthony greeted us with a few beers. He put his arm around Collin and led him to another room while I sat with Rocky at the table. I noticed Boss, Guido, and Three Fingers were missing. I asked Rocky where everyone was and he assured me not to worry, they'd be around in a minute. They were just showing Collin around the restaurant, getting to know him. I sat and drank two beers with Rocky, not realizing how much time was passing.

A few moments later, Collin walked out followed by Boss, Anthony, Guido, and Three Fingers and his face was as pale as a ghost! They offered us another beer but we had to get going. Collin shook their hands and Anthony wiped on his shirt as if Collin's hands were wet.

As we walked across the street and got in the car, I could see sweat dripping from his brow. I asked him if he was okay and Collin told me what he experienced.

He had a frustrated tone and said "I had no idea I was going to be interrogated by the mob when you told me your friends wanted to meet me. . . "

I looked at him concerned, I had no idea that was the plan!

"I'm taking you home right after the dance. No after parties, no camp outs, no cemetery chugs, just straight home."

I was so confused! We always had plans for after the dances!

Collin could see my confusion and then told me the rest of his story.

"It was as if a light switched, they went from welcoming me in their restaurant and then circled around me in a dark room! They started asking me what my intentions are with you for tonight!"

"Well, what did you tell them!?" I asked anxiously.

"I told them 'Nothing! 'and the Boss said 'That's right, Collin! Nothing! You will go to the dance with Sheila, and you will come back. That is it. You see, Sheila is our friend, more like our daughter, and Guido here will be very upset if anything happens to Sheila. So, enjoy yourself at the dance and then bring her safely home.'"

He was visibly shaken up. I tried hard not to giggle under my concerned look. I took their message very seriously, but knew they were exaggerating the fear of God in Collin a bit.

We went to the dance, but I don't think Collin had any fun. He seemed a little paranoid as if someone was watching him the whole night. The moment the final song ended he dragged me to the car and took me home. He walked me to the door and said goodnight.

I never went on another date with him again!

# CHAPTER 8

---

# Mourning the Innocent

While every death is tragic, my father knew it was also part of the life cycle.

We treated every loss as if it was from within our own family. We supported them emotionally however we could, and we would serve them to the best of our abilities to ensure their loved one was remembered and honored in a beautifully meaningful manner.

However, there were a few delicate conditions where my father didn't believe the families should pay for our services.

The first was the death of a newborn child.

At the time, stillborn wakes were unheard of. The thought of providing a full wake and burial service for a child who hadn't had a moment to grasp their lives fully was unthinkable.

We wanted to provide a memorable send-off for those little loves, again as we would for our own families.

We brought in several tiny white caskets, lined with the softest, most luscious interior for stillborn children. The parents, grandparents, and other immediate family members would meet at the funeral home and have a proper moment to grieve their sudden loss. A priest or religious person would also be invited to say a few prayers.

The caskets would usually remain closed, but the families could discuss if they desired to see the child one last time. They would also have an opportunity to place loving gifts in the casket to be buried with their infant before we would all journey to the cemetery.

The baby would ride in the hearse and the family would have the option to follow along in their own cars or be driven in a limo.

It was a full-service wake and funeral for their little love's immediate family members and gave them the chance to find a sense of closure in this unforeseen, and unimaginable, experience.

My parents believed no one should have to bury their child, and couldn't imagine the emotional toll and physical shock of experiencing a stillborn death. They didn't believe the parents should be burdened with the costs associated with this tragedy.

Unfortunately, these funerals became more and more common as the years went on. Baby lives were taken as lives were at any age. I would do my best to avoid looking into the eyes of these parents because their sorrow was so deep that I often felt the strength of their emotions and loss myself. I tended to remain quieter on these days.

The second condition was the death of a public servant lost in the line of duty.

While my parents were incredibly generous and were always hosting or donating to fundraisers for everything from orphanages in Peru to feeding the homeless in Chicago and more, they also believed in supporting those who give their lives to support us on a daily basis.

My dad believed they put their lives on the line for us and the least we could do was bury them for free. It was always such a sad and hard day when we knew the wake and funeral was for a fallen police officer, firefighter, or EMT.

Everything from flowers to the grave was donated. Officers, Firefighters, and EMTs would come from all over the state and, depending on the cause of death, sometimes from around the country. It was like the changing of the guard surrounding the caskets. They would take turns honoring their fallen comrade and guarding their body.

There's one service that still remains clear in my mind to this day. This police officer had a wife, three children, and one of his children was a newborn. He died in the line of duty by being shot in the face. Unfortunately, that meant it had to be a closed casket. I had never seen so many Police Officers in the same room. There were so many wanting to guard their fallen brother that the changing of the guards occurred every 30 minutes instead of the traditional hour.

As the wake continued to grow, one of his comrades realized that all of these officers wouldn't have a chance to stand guard of the casket. So, he gathered some paper, walked to the front of the room, stood just beside the casket, and made an announcement to the room.

"We are here today to honor our fallen brother, and serve him as he served all of us. If you would like to volunteer your service to his wife and his three children, please take a moment to sign up to cut their grass, or remove snow, or make a meal, or clean their car so that his family can have the support they need during this challenging time."

This was above and beyond anything I had ever seen before. His young widow cried in appreciation as one by one the officers and their families approached the signup sheets and chose days, or even weeks, to help her and her family with anything they could think of. I heard that a lot of police officers came and painted her entire home, too, to help lighten her atmosphere.

By the end of the day, they had filled up those sheets to help with countless chores and necessities for a full year.

Those wakes were some of the saddest, and some of the largest we held. Hundreds and hundreds of people would come to pay their respects.

We would have to have ropes and stanchions to keep people in line, and we would snake that through the parking lot because of the sheer number of people. Police would be directing traffic. We would need parking across the street at the bowling alley that held about 100 cars between that parking lot and the food store parking lot.

The day of the funeral always started hours before the family came. Most of the time, TV and radio were there to have live coverage of the funeral. And the number of police cars would line up for blocks and blocks. Most would go before the hearse and then followed by more police cars. All with their sirens on. All traffic would stop or pull off to the side, and as the first police cars would be pulling into the cemetery miles away, the last cars would be pulling out of the funeral home parking lot.

I always thought it was a true testament to this fallen warrior who gave up their life for us to live ours.

For police, there would be a 21 gun salute at the cemetery.

For firefighters, the casket would be transported on the fallen heroes fire truck. When we would walk outside the building, there would be fire trucks from other firehouses, with their ladders raised, and the American flag would be hanging from the two ladders of the trucks.

The casket would be placed on the fire truck of the firehouse, and just like the police, the fire trucks would lead the procession with their lights and sirens on.

Mayors from all over would be at the funeral. And if the fallen hero had children, usually the school would send their class to the funeral on a school bus.

The funerals for these horrible tragedies were so well attended that it would take more than half a day from beginning to end.

Sometimes, the families would be so in shock at the number of people that they would get completely lost or overwhelmed at the moment. Therefore, we started videotaping those services so that the widows and loved ones left behind could remember the day and have another moment to process that day. Even if it took them years to look at the video or never looked at it, at least they had it to view.

I have such respect for all these people in uniform. Making the choice to run into a burning building or run into a gunfight to save the lives of others instead of running away to protect themselves is unimaginable to me. Their camaraderie and commitment to their families, friends, co-workers, neighbors, or strangers they will never meet was always an impressive thing to experience.

These days inspired me to always show my gratitude for anyone in a uniform. I still do. If I'm at an airport and I see police or firefighters or military members, I do my best to thank them and, if possible, pay for what they are eating if we are at a restaurant or a coffee if we are in line. I have seen the risks that they are taking too many times to not.

These traumatic moments have lived with me for many years and have helped make me the person I am today. They helped me open my eyes to harsh realities in our lives and the sacrifices, hardships, and hurdles we will all encounter at one point or another.

And, most importantly, these painfully clear memories have drilled into my head every single day and night of my life that nothing is guaranteed.

Life is a gift, meant to be lived and enjoyed and loved, and shared because we don't have a clue what the coming hours, days, months, or years will bring.

When people say be grateful for everything, I know I am.

When people say enjoy every second, I know I do.

I love life, and I'm thankful that all these families allowed me to be a part of their most challenging times in their life because it taught me how to truly appreciate mine.

# CHAPTER 9

---

# The Ten Rules of the Tinkers

I was 13 years old at this time, and my father had me working professionally at the funeral home for six years in one way or another, and to be honest, I thought I had seen everything. However, I wasn't prepared at all for the group that was about to walk into the foyer.

A family of young brothers and sisters walked into the funeral home and said their mother died. It was clear they were travelers, tinkers, gypsies. They dressed a little eccentric for our small Catholic town in the southwest suburbs of Chicago, making it clear that if they weren't gypsies, they were at least a little free-spirited. These teenagers approached one of our secretaries and asked if we would be willing to host a service for their mom.

You may be thinking to yourself of course, any funeral home would help a family who has just lost a loved one. However, for gypsies at this time, this wasn't the case. Many funeral homes wouldn't serve them because, as travelers, they normally came from far distances and wouldn't always be able to find places where they could stay together. When they came to town for wakes and services, they usually wanted to sleep in the funeral home, barbecue in the parking lot and more.

This wasn't my father's first visit with them. The secretary excused herself to my father's office, where I was sitting in the corner. She explained the situation, and my father turned to the secretary and said, "I know who these people are; I will handle this. The head of their family is called the King of the Tinkers." I giggled, and he gave me a stern look.

He came out from his office and went up to the teens and simply said: "I want to talk to the King." They reluctantly left, and my father began scribbling a long list of rules he wanted them to follow, thinking of everything that might go wrong that he could prevent.

About an hour later, a group of 15 people walked through the front door of the funeral home, led by their King.

Their King was a tall but scrawny looking older gentleman. He was dressed in canvas pants and a white button down shirt with a colorfully embroidered vest. He wore a loosely fitted hat that had floppy edges, and was covered in feather accessories. He was the oldest of the group, and you could tell he was either well respected, or completely feared by this group. Everyone was looking to him for guidance on how to proceed.

The stereotypes and ideas that come to mind when someone is referred to as a "Gypsy" have grown and adapted over time, but in my experience, I will always associate my understanding of their culture through their wakes and funerals. If we want to start by getting technical, in the Merriam-Webster's Dictionary, a Gypsy (n.) is known as "a nomadic and free-spirited person."

Well, if you have ever attended a Gypsy funeral, you would know that this definition is quite agreeable because this ceremony became one of the most memorable services we had ever hosted in the history of our family's business!

My father welcomed them, expressed his condolences, and led the group into one of the arrangement rooms. The arrangement rooms are where the families go to discuss the specifics of the service. Everything from day and time to flowers and casket and cremation or burial are discussed and decided upon. It takes a few hours to get everything squared away. Usually, there are only a few people, immediate family members. So, as you can imagine, these rooms are relatively small. Nevertheless, this group of 18 people, the gypsies, their King, my father, and I paraded over to the first arrangement room, squeezed in, and shut the door.

My father had brought me in with him to write everything down. Once everyone was situated, my father and the King sat at the desk across from one another. On the desk was a piece of paper, and my father said, "I'm going to have my daughter read this list. If you agree to it, we will bury your loved one, and I would like you to sign it." They nodded yes, and my father turned, looked at me and said, "Sheila, read the list."

I looked around the room at everyone staring at me, took a deep breath, and began.

You must use the bathrooms, no defecating in the parking lot

You cannot sleep in the funeral

You cannot take anything out of the funeral home

You cannot camp out in the parking lot

You cannot inappropriately touch any employees

You cannot cook in the parking lot

You cannot bury anything in the casket with your loved one, dead or alive

You will be provided with a large waking room; please respect the others in the building and stay in your room as they will stay in their room

We have a coffee room you can use

You must pay in cash before we provide these services for your loved one

If any of these rules are broken, you will have to pay for any restitutions

My father then turned his attention back to the King and directly asked: "Well, is this acceptable to you?"

The King had a minor eye exchange with his family and said yes.

Happily, my father exclaimed, "Great! Please sign here and I'll take this paper with me."

The King signed his name, and my father stood, thanked the group for their understanding, assured them there would be a wonderful service for their loved one, and began to walk out. "My job here is done, and Sheila will make the rest of the arrangements with you from this point on."

My eyes darted over to my father's, and my heart started to pound, loud enough that I'm sure the group could tell I was a little nervous. I thought to myself "You're going to leave me alone with them? Thanks a lot, Dad."

While I had conducted hundreds of these meetings before, I was still a little anxious. After hearing all of this, I didn't know what to expect. However, as the conversations continued I discovered they were really loving and nice people. My anxiety quickly faded as I learned more about their lives and culture. It was very interesting and it taught me a lot about first impressions in general. I was thankful for the chance to be proven wrong, and for the opportunity to see their culture in action, even though it wasn't the happiest occasion.

The wake was going to occur in two days to give people time to make the journey to the wake.

My mom and father had left for a few days which they did every now and then to get away and regroup. We were always very busy and they just needed to pick up and leave, or they would go insane. This was one of those times. My father told me before their trip to prepare for anything and everything. I wasn't sure what to expect, but I guessed that was the point, to expect the unexpected. And boy, was he right.

They came all the way from TX, FL, CA, WI, IN, TN, and many more states. Our huge parking lot that fit over 100 cars was utterly packed with RVs and large trucks and trucks with trailers. It seemed to me many of them lived in these vehicles as their full-time home, not just for vacations.

The night before the wake, I was up late preparing for whatever madness was about to begin. The funeral home had been closed for a few hours, and it took me almost that amount of time to set up the spaces for the wake. I finally went upstairs to go to sleep. I could hear a lot of commotion outside because my bedroom window faced one side of the parking lot. It was the minor part of the lot. The larger area was behind the building. I got out of bed and looked out the window. I didn't see anything out of place but decided it would be good to look around. I went out our back door, onto the roof of the funeral home, and looked out over the larger section of parking lot, and I could see all the RVs lined up with large crowds of people, tents, and chairs set up with BBQs going and more. They were breaking several of the rules my father and I had shared with them. I quickly ran into the house, thanking God that my parents had left the phone number to the hotel they were staying at.

I rang the hotel, "Mr. Lamb's room, please."

"Do you know what time it is?" The receptionist asked. That's back when we had "respectable" times to call.

"Yes," I said. "I know what time it is, and it's an emergency; now please connect me to his room."

I could almost see her eyes rolling in disapproval as she confirmed she would connect me.

Ring, ring.

My father finally answered, sounding groggy and tired. Before he could even get a complete word out I blurted out, "Hello Dad, it's me; we have a problem. All the gypsies are camping out in the funeral home parking lot and are cooking, drinking, and more!"

"Are the embalmers still working?"

"No, they left at midnight. It's two in the morning."

He sighed and hesitatingly said, "I hate to ask you to do this, but can you go out there and ask to speak to the King? Tell the King I want to talk to him now and call me back here. I'll tell the receptionist to put you right through. Use the phone in the flower room, it's the closest to the back parking lot."

As my voice began shaking, I responded "Okay, call you in a few."

I put on my robe and slippers, dragged a brush through my hair and looked at myself in the mirror and said, "Sheila, you can do this. It will all be okay."

I went downstairs and ran to the back door. It was one of those eerily dark nights, and my anxiety was heightened. I took a moment to get rid of the shakes, unlocked the back door, and proceeded to walk out into this late night block party. I walked through the crowds, greeting everyone nicely and asking where the King was.

"Hello, do you know where the King is? No? Maybe that way? Okay, thank you."

"Hello, hello, hi hi. Do you know where the King is?"

I continued to snake my way through the crowd of tractors, trailers, RVs and people. I couldn't believe the police hadn't been called with how loud it was, everyone talking, playing music, singing and so on. It was just wild. If I hadn't been working at the funeral home, and trying to sleep, I probably would have enjoyed spending time there, myself. After about fifteen minutes of searching I found the King.

I greeted him and sternly requested that he come with me to speak with my father.

He understood and followed me to the flower room. After speaking to the same receptionist, I was put right through to my father.

I passed the phone to the King and heard my father loudly through the phone "You call yourself the King of the Tinkers but you're going back on your word. I have a piece of paper here in my hand that you yourself signed saying you would not sleep in the parking lot, cook or anything and Sheila told me the parking lot is full?"

The King responded calmly "Yes, Matt it is. This whole new group had a long journey and just arrived. They wanted to gather together after so much time apart."

My father said, "You know that legally I can't have them there. If anything happens to anyone I don't have insurance for any of this. You will need to find other accommodation tonight or we will not have the burial tomorrow. Now you're the King, tell your family what to do."

The King agreed, understanding that the situation wasn't personal but necessary.

My father told the King he would call me back in a half hour to see how it was handled and would check in again tomorrow. They hung up the phone, and the King went back out.

It took about an hour to get everyone out of there, but they did move. I finally got to sleep around 4:00 AM when all was well. My father didn't check back in that night, as he probably assumed I would call if there were any other issues. Thank goodness there weren't!

The next morning the parking lot began to fill up again as they started migrating back to the funeral home for the wake.

The phones were always ringing at the funeral home, and this morning was no different. As everyone was answering phones and preparing for the gypsy funeral, I picked up one of the ringing lines.

"This is Sheila, how can I help you?"

"Yes, This is Father O'Brien."

"Oh yes. Hi Father, how are you?"

"Fine, but we had a very unusual night here. There were about 100 or so gypsies parked in our parking lot. They said they were going to your place this morning. They were BBQing and singing, I didn't know what to do! It was about 3:00 in the morning so I let them stay."

"Really?!" I replied in shock, with my jaw dropping the more he talked. But I had to make sure everything was all right.

"I guess they must have been confused as to where to go in the middle of the night. Are they all gone?"

"Yes, Sheila, they are. But I have to inquire, they will not be staying tonight, right?"

"Oh no Father, their funeral is today and they will all leave from the cemetery." I wasn't actually sure what their plan was tonight, but to my knowledge there was no other reason for them to stay another night.

"Good to hear, have a blessed day, Sheila."

"You too, Father."

I hung up the phone and burst out into laughter and tears. At least Father O'Brien was nice enough to let them stay, and is a very forgiving person!

The services came and went. It was a busy day that seemed to whizz past me and everyone else. We were all exhausted and word had spread about the night before, so we were also wondering what else to expect. We seemed to have made it through the day without a hitch, and we were almost ready to breathe a sigh of relief. The finish line was getting closer, and the strangest service I had ever participated in was almost over.

The closing prayers had begun and, as usual, everyone passed the casket for a last look, prayer, touch. Usually the immediate family, mostly around 5-10 people, stays for the closing of the casket just a bit longer after everyone else. For this closing there were about 30 people. I remember thinking to myself, "this is a really large family."

The funeral director made his way to the front of the viewing room and began to close the casket. Some of the women that were in the room were wailing and crying loudly. They started yelling words and noises at one another. My colleagues and I started looking at each other incredibly confused.

One woman ran to the casket before it was completely shut and put an oversized, fire engine red, rotary phone in the casket.

She slowly backed away and let out an "OK, it's OK."

The funeral director started to close the casket again and heard another woman scream "Wait! Wait!" Now what? The woman ran to the casket and took the phone off the hook. Paused for a moment, then put the phone back on the hook. Everyone began talking and yelling in another language, and it seemed that they had finally agreed to leave the phone off the hook.

The funeral director looked at me, then looked around the room as if he was preparing for someone else to hurl themselves towards the casket. But what came next we could have never guessed.

Moments later, someone ran into the room with a live chicken. Yes, you read that correctly, a live chicken! They threw this chicken into the casket, and the funeral director jumped back in fear and confusion. I can't imagine how he felt as this person was running towards him yelling with a live chicken, that was also going absolutely berserk.

Now, everyone started going out of their minds and began screaming along with the chicken. The women were wailing, my colleagues were trying to capture this chicken, and most of the bystanders were gasping out of shock and laughing out of disbelief.

The family began to clap and yell in agreement to leave the chicken in the casket. The funeral director was trying to have the family step back so he could remove the chicken loudly explaining why he can't let the chicken be buried with the deceased woman. "No! "We can not bury this live chicken with her, we will not allow it! You must remove the chicken!"

The poor chicken was squawking and screaming and flapping its wings. The man who brought the chicken took out a massive knife to cut the chicken's head off. Now I began to scream as this was absolutely terrifying!

He moved the funeral director aside, grabbed the chicken by the neck, brought it over to a table, laid it down and lifted the knife way above his head. The group was cheering him on, crying, screaming, wailing, and the chicken was obviously going mad and completely distressed, fearing it was about to die, too.

The funeral director had completely lost control of the room and I was frozen in disbelief.

All of the sudden, my father walked in and yelled as loud as he could, "STOP! STOP EVERYTHING RIGHT NOW! PUT THE KNIFE DOWN NOW! PUT THE CHICKEN DOWN! EVERYONE COMPOSE YOURSELVES!"

We all turned and the room went silent, except for the chicken who was still in fear of its life.

My father walked over to the King and said, "No chickens, dead or alive in the casket. Do you understand?"

The King simply shook his head and replied, "Yes."

The funeral director made his way back to the casket, and began to slowly shut it once more. One last attempt was made by this man to put the chicken in the casket, which sent my father off the edge. "GET THAT CHICKEN OUT OF THIS BUILDING!"

The crying, wailing, yelling, clapping continued on in the background as the chicken was escorted out of the chapel.

My father walked up to the casket and yelled over all of the noise "Close this casket and get them to the cemetery! This is over!"

They finally closed the casket, put the casket in the hearse, went to the cemetery, had the closing prayers and we were done. There were miles of RVs, tractor trailers, and vans all parked and ready to stay awhile in the cemetery. I thought wow, I bet they will be here for days.

As everything was coming to a close, and the rooms were being cleaned and prepped for the next day of services, I sat down with my father at his desk. "I thought you were staying away another night?"

My father said, "I figured today would be a fiasco so we came back. We didn't want to miss out on all of the fun!"

The next day, the King came into the funeral home, I saw him and greeted him. He said, "Before I leave, I would like to speak to your father. I have something for him."

I nodded and went to fetch him. He was upstairs in our apartment, so I called him and said, "Dad, the King is here to talk to you."

"Oh great," my father, sarcastically. "This should be interesting."

He came downstairs and the King presented him with a box wrapped in newspapers. My father opened it and inside was a framed picture of an old time gypsy wagon with my father's pictures in the window of the wagon. On top of the picture they wrote, "Matt Lamb, King of the Tinkers!"

My father and the King laughed hard. The King finally broke their laughter by saying "You are now a part of us, you are family and we thank you, Matt."

They hugged, and had a last laugh looking at the picture, then both went their own ways. My father hung that picture with pride in our kitchen. When we moved he took it with him and put it in his bedroom. He really cherished their interaction and knew he would see them again.

This whole experience was a life lesson for me as I had never had any interaction with gypsies before this. This service exposed me to so many aspects of their lives from their love and respect for each other, their way of dressing, their manner of talking, and their unique cuisines. I found it exciting and different at the same time. Although everyone grieves, people can and do process death in very different ways.

As long as the chickens get to live.

# CHAPTER 10

---

# Funeral Home Etiquette

"I lived above a funeral home."

That sentence alone seems to stop people in their tracks.

"You mean, it's like an apartment building and there's a funeral home on the first floor?"

"Nope."

"You mean, like on a hill and the funeral home is at the bottom of the hill?"

"Nope." This isn't like the movie *Psycho* okay?!

"There's one building, with three floors. Kind of like a house. Your house has bedrooms on the top floor, a living room on the main floor where you host family and friends, and you have storage in the basement.

That's like my house!

The top floor is where we sleep, the main floor is where we host everyone, and the basement is for storage." Without going into too many details. . . the top floor was our apartment, the main floor was the chapel, and the basement was where we stored and embalmed the bodies.

See! My house was just like yours!

Although, we did have a few other chores to consider in order to make our house function properly.

So here's your introduction to our processes:

How to operate a funeral home:

### Rule 1. Keep your cool.

Literally. I'll never forget the harsh summers. Those were always tough for us to handle because of the design of our building.

The sun would beat down on the flat roofs and it would make the building hotter than hell. With so many people coming in and out, the AC wouldn't be enough to keep the building cool. As a result, Matt and I would have to wake up before 6:00 AM, before anyone else arrived, and before it would be too hot for us to be on the roof, and prepare the roofs for the day. Matt and I would have to soak massive white sheets in cold water and hang them around the roof to cool down the exterior of the building. We would completely soak these sheets and leave them hanging, continuing watering them down to cool the building, sometimes even throwing bags of ice across them.

The sheets would be removed before morning wakes or funerals began for the day and once they were finished we would put them back up again before the afternoon services began. It might seem like an extremely primitive solution, but it surprisingly worked! And it worked well!

As you can probably imagine from all of my stories, working at this funeral home was an interesting experience for the employees as well, not just for our family. If my parents were willing to work Matt and me to the ground everyday for nothing, you can imagine what was expected of the workers there who were paid! Work ethic and work environments were so different then. When I look back it amazes me to see how different business environments can be now. How flexible they can be.

### Rule 2. Brush it off.

When I think back to the winters when I lived there, I always remember there being more snow, in larger amounts, for longer periods of time than there is now. In the 60s and 70s, it felt as if winter never ended! We would get little tidbits of spring, and a splash of summer, before a hint of fall and then drown in frozen blizzards!

The building was large, and had three different levels of roofs. What made snow difficult to deal with was the fact that all of the roofs were flat. This meant if they held a lot of snow there was the possibility of the roofs collapsing.

Therefore, when heavy snow would come, my parents would tell Matt and I to invite our friends over to climb up on snowy ladders with heavy shovels and clear off the roofs! While it was fun the first time or two, this could go on for months. Sometimes, we would have to do this daily, or even three times a day depending on the storm!

Luckily, we had our own snow removal truck for the parking lot. During snow storms someone would be driving it several times throughout the night to make sure the parking lot would stay clear. Then early in the morning Matt and I would pop up on the roofs before any guests would arrive and it would be removed too. But sometimes, it would have to wait for an hour or so. On weekends, this would make for some very high and enjoyable hills of snow we could ride our sleds down! It was certainly a bittersweet experience. Most days at least. Sometimes it was just bitterly freezing.

### Rule 3. Don't die with debt.

As I continued to grow up I took on more responsibilities, all of which I was never paid for. And those responsibilities included paying the employees.

Every Friday morning, I would be woken up around 5:30 AM by my dad yelling, "Sheila, it's Friday!"

Normally, students were excited for Fridays, right? The excitement of the weekend coming and all that jazz. Not me! Friday meant something completely different in my mind.

At about 5:35 AM I would finally muster up the energy to crawl out of bed. Usually because that first notice was followed by a second reminder. "SHEILA! FRIDAY!"

I would get out of bed, grab my robe and fill the giant dog bowl with dry food. I would wait for Smokey to finish devouring his bowl and open the back door to let him out onto the deck. Then I would begin the paycheck system.

On the dining table would be a stack of checks and a stack of window envelopes. Each one had to be folded and stuffed into an envelope, and there weren't just five or ten of these, there were probably close to sixty or seventy. All of them had to be finished and sealed and delivered to their appropriate mailbox by 6:00 AM. Even if no one was at work by 8:00 AM, we had a few runners that would transport checks to our other branches all over the Chicagoland area. The runners would arrive by 6:15 AM so they could have the checks delivered in time for the employees at the other branches. I understood that they all needed their pay on Friday, but I didn't understand why it would matter if they got it at 7:00 AM or at 12:00 PM. Either way, I got it done in time.

It also felt a little scandalous for me to see all of their paychecks. I found out when people got raises, when they got vacation pay, or when they got demotions. I remember looking through their checks and always surprised by the amounts they were paid. I would have expected more pay for some jobs and less for others, but their wide ranges always kept me interested.

Holidays and birthdays were even busier on Friday mornings!

For each employee's birthday, they got a card and a small gift card to a local restaurant or store with a bonus check.

For Thanksgiving, everyone received a frozen turkey (which I didn't have to deliver, thankfully) and a nice bottle of whiskey with a card to their family.

For Christmas, each person got a second check for the same amount as their normal check with a "Merry Christmas" card from my parents.

But in election years, those were the icing on the cake! The week before elections, my dad would give me a stack of handwritten notes to put in each envelope, and every year it was the same message.

"We are Americans, and as an American, it is our privilege to vote. This is our duty, and as our duty, I expect you to vote. You can vote before, during, or after work. You can vote for anyone you want to. Write in Mickey Mouse for all I care, but you must vote. I will check to make sure you voted. So, if this message wasn't clear enough for you here it is blatantly:

If you want to see your paycheck next week, I suggest you exercise your right as an American and vote."

The first time I saw this and put the message in the envelope, I was shocked!

If we live in a free country, it is our choice to vote, right? Personally, I couldn't wait to vote, but I wondered if everyone thought that. My dad had instilled a sense of American pride in my ability to vote as an American, and as a woman, it wasn't always this way.

I usually didn't pry on these kinds of matters, but one year I decided to ask if anyone had ever not voted.

He sat straight up as if he was proud of himself and smiled as he turned to me and said: "So far, every election year, everyone has voted."

I always found that week of the election year incredibly exciting and found his belief in our ability as normal, everyday, people to create change inspiring.

While he might have been inspiring to some, there were certainly others who despised him. And not only him, but his father as well, who owned the funeral home before my father did.

One in particular, was the janitor, Bob.

This story has foundations which go all the way back to my grandfather.

My grandfather, Matthew James, was what they called a gentleman's gentleman, which means he was always coiffed to the fullest. He wore a clean pressed suit, with his hair slicked back, and shined his shoes daily. He spoke properly, and professionally at all times and never lost his temper. He drank gin martinis everyday and walked around with Pepto Bismol in one pocket, and Listerine in the other, never knowing what to expect throughout the day. He was always the optimist, and here's one of my favorite stories he shared.

When my dad was a child, his siblings, my grandfather, and his wife Margaret, all lived above one of the first few funeral homes from the chain. Not the one I lived above, but I guess you could say living with death became a Lamb family tradition.

They went to church every Sunday as a family. It was *the* place to see and be seen. It was also customary during that time to go out for brunch after Sunday mass. It was like a Catholic block party every week, all of the families would attend and catch up and spend time together enjoying a meal after their prayers.

One Sunday, while the family was sitting down about to eat, a few members of the parish began approaching my grandfather and suggested he head back to the funeral home.

"Matthew James, you might want to go back, it seems like something is wrong at your place. . . "

My grandfather told me he was concerned, but not overly worried. What could be wrong at a funeral home on a Sunday, he thought?

After a few more parishioners made the same comment, he decided it would be a good idea to check on the funeral home and see what all of the commotion was about.

When he pulled up to the front of the funeral home he noticed immediately that the front door were wide open and all of the lights were on, and he had left just a few hours earlier with the door locked and the lights off.

He slowly exited his car and began to scan the building in awe, and completely baffled.

I know what you're thinking, poltergeists, right?

Across all of the windows in the front said in bright red paint:

"SCREW YOU MR. LAMB. I QUIT!"

He knew it could be only one person. The one person with keys to the front door. The one person who knew where the paint was stored. The one person who obviously hated my grandfather, Bob the janitor.

My grandfather was somewhat in shock, but also somewhat amused. He arranged for the front of the building to be cleaned that afternoon and went about his business.

A few days later, Bob showed up to pick up his last check and as he was leaving he turned around and yelled at my grandfather "Hah! How'd you like my message, huh!? I sure showed you!"

"Oh no, Bob. You were very respectful!"

"WHAT?! Respectful? I don't respect you!"

"Oh yes you do! You called me *Mister* Lamb!"

Bob was furious and was escorted out of the building by security screaming at my grandfather the whole way out. He never came back, or left any other messages.

Personally, I don't know who taught lessons on respect better, my grandfather or Aretha Franklin. Either way, Bob entered into an intensive course that day! One he won't ever forget!

# CHAPTER 11

———

# Leather, Liquor, and Lookouts

Have you ever seen a big, burly, sturdy, muscular, rugged man sob?

Have you ever seen a room of big, burly, sturdy, muscular, rugged men collapse in sadness?

This is the effect that death has on all of us, but when you put that image of a large man and hundreds of his beefy comrades in a room surrounding a casket, wearing all black with bandanas, leather boots, with leather jackets shouting the Harley Davidson logo on it, and covered in chains, you instantly became aware of a couple of things.

You never knew what to expect when there was a death in a biker gang.

You knew it was about to get rowdy.

Well, after years of experience our family knew how to organize these wakes and funerals so that everything usually went fine during these services. However, there were still a few occasions where we would worry a little extra.

There was one time where that little extra worry became a hurricane of fury, fear, and passion and I remember it like it was yesterday.

My dad and I were sitting in his office reviewing the upcoming services when his secretary knocked on the door. She popped her head around and nervously whispered "Mr. Lamb, there is someone here to see you."

Now, we have seen deaths from all kinds of groups, for all kinds of people, from all cultures. Everyone dies. So the fact that she was a little nervous piqued my attention. I was curious as to who could have instilled this uneasiness in her for what appeared to be a routine consultation.

We stood up and my father said "Sure, let them in."

When she opened the door the largest amount of black leather I had ever seen walked through the door under a massive beard and dark sunglasses.

He reached out his hand towards my father and said "Mr. Lamb, it's a pleasure, I'm Jack."

"Hello Jack, please have a seat. This is my daughter, Sheila. The world's first and best child undertaker. How can we help you today?"

Now I began to understand why his secretary was on edge. The last time we had a biker gang wake, a rival biker gang showed up and caused a lot of trouble. They slashed the tires and damaged the bikes, one time they even started shooting as people were exiting the building.

We made the mistake once of not having police officers present, and learned very quickly that from that point on we needed protection for our clients, the grieving visitors, and our employees.

He spoke low and somberly, "We've had a death in the family. Our brother, John."

We expressed our condolences and offered our support. We learned that John had been shot and killed by a member of a rival biker gang. We also learned that John had a brother in jail at the time and another brother wanted by the F.B.I.

Jack asked that aside from the normal services we provided, if we could help arrange for John's brother who was in jail, Dom, to be let out on furlough for a visitation. My father agreed to try, but couldn't promise anything.

Our family believed everyone had a right to grieve, and a wake or funeral service is part of the grieving process. It offered closure to families and loved ones, or friends and neighbors to heal in a small way.

As we always said, funerals are for the living, not the dead.

After further discussion Jack left and we agreed we would talk in a day or two to discuss logistics if John's brother could attend.

The second Jack closed the door I turned to my father and asked

"Okay, it's a gang shooting. How many police officers should I request?"

Gang shootings always brought out a lot of people. And Jack seemed to be one of the gang leaders, which meant John was a pretty important member.

We decided to discuss complete logistics once we learned if John's brother, Dom, could attend.

My father got on the phone with the jail and, to our surprise, they agreed to let Dom come. However, they had a strict set of rules for us to follow.

Dom would arrive one hour before the public, and only have one hour to be there. He would only be allowed in the room with his mother, and there would be several police officers from the prison surveilling him. They would arrive in an armored car, and he would be wearing his prisoner uniform. No suit, no tie. Just his normal everyday, locked up, gear. No one else could be allowed to be in the room, or the foyer, while this was in process, and they needed a direct exit to remove him if any chaos were to occur, such as an attempt to flee, or a gang disturbance of any kind.

We agreed to the precautions, and said we would ensure that all of this was taken into account.

The next day the news of John's death became public knowledge and the F.B.I. contacted my father right away.

"Mr. Lamb, we have learned that the brother of one of our warrants has died and that you are holding his wake and funeral service. Is that correct?"

"Yes, it is."

"Mr. Lamb, we'd like to send two of our professional agents to pose as workers at the funeral in case our warrant makes an appearance."

"Doesn't that sound a little extreme? His brother just died, can you find out where they are eating after?"

"Mr. Lamb, you don't really have a choice in the matter. We will be there that morning. We won't bug you, or bother you, you won't even know who the agents are, but just know we will be there and if the warrant shows up, we will arrest him."

My father hung up the phone, and said "Well, this won't be the best move for business, but I can't tell the F.B.I. what they can and can't do!"

I sarcastically exclaimed "What!? Why not?! Don't they know who they're talking to!"

We laughed it off a bit, but were still concerned with how that would play out.

Two days later it was the day of John's service.

My father and I were up at the crack of dawn to prepare for what we were sure was about to be an eventful day. We arranged the largest visitation chapel we had, laid out the prayer cards and the sign in books. We also set up the flowers around the casket, which were not the normal choice of color. Typically, flowers that surround a casket are white, or representative of something the deceased loved, such as a sports team or their favorite color. But for John, they were mostly black and red. Additionally, they had a full Harley Davidson floral arrangement, their gang's patch, and a big gun made out of red and purple carnations. Setting those oversized floral sculptures up was a bit of an undertaking, but we made it work.

Next, we prepared the casket with a few more flower decorations and ensured that John looked as normal as he could, considering what he had suffered. I remember they chose a very specific outfit for him. His full biker gang uniform. He was wearing dark jeans, a Harley Davidson shirt, his leather vest with his gang's patches covering it from top to bottom, finished off with his red and black bandana, his sunglasses perched on his forehead and his black leather riding gloves with his hands clasped across his stomach. Usually, families choose to have their loved one buried in their finest clothes. But this outfit, we could tell, was more special to John, his family and his gang.

That morning was similar to the beginning of almost any service, aside from a few extra jobs to take care of after our normal procedures.

It was suggested to us by the prison that we should set up a few precautions for Dom's visitation. So, this morning, aside from our normal duties we had police officers arrive at

6:00 AM and scheduled to have security on the property until 10:00 AM the next day. We greeted the officers, made them some coffee and discussed the logistics of the day ahead. Additionally, we set a curtain in front of the emergency exit in the back corner of the chapel so that it wasn't fully visible, but it did not impede the guards' access to it. We didn't want to entice Dom to attempt to flee. Additionally, since this was our largest chapel, and it was actually a few rooms put together, we locked all of the exits from the other spaces, and left only one door unlocked to enter and exit the room from the foyer.

We had no idea what to expect during this visitation, but figured that Dom simply wanted to pay his respects, grieve, and find closure.

However, we also learned through our conversation with Jack that Dom's presence would be a little controversial for the family. Therefore, we also wanted to ensure that the rest of the family hadn't arrived yet, so we arranged for Dom to arrive at 7:00 AM and set the wake to begin at 9:00 AM. That gave us plenty of time to ensure Dom was on his way back to prison, and his mother would have a few moments to gather herself before the rest of the visitors would arrive.

John's mother pulled in around 6:45 AM. She walked into the chapel as we were setting up the last few elements of John's casket. We welcomed her, expressed our condolences, offered her refreshments, as we would for anyone who was grieving and invited her to approach the casket. She asked for coffee, and asked if she could wait for Dom in the chapel. She didn't want to see him in an armored truck. We agreed. Before I exited the chapel I could hear her begin to quietly sob. She hesitatingly walked up to the casket, almost as if she didn't believe John would be there, and breathed a deep sigh of sadness. She brushed John's head, told him how stupid he was for getting himself shot, but that she still loved him. Then she turned around, moved to the front row of the chapel and sat quietly waiting for Dom.

She was a small, frail woman. She wore all black, as a grieving mother usually does, with a nice long coat and a black hat with a veil to cover her face. She seemed fairly normal. More normal than I would have expected with the family she had.

My father and I stood in our lobby by the front door at 6:55 AM waiting for Dom. At exactly 6:59 AM an armored truck pulled into our driveway.

Dom exited the truck in a bright orange prisoner's suit, with full chains on his wrists and ankles connected to his waist and guided by two armed officers, who each held one of his arms as they walked towards the lobby. When they all walked in I remember thinking to myself:

"Holy crap, this is real. This is a real prisoner, with real guards, and he's really locked in shackles. Holy CRAP!"

My father welcomed Dom and the officers to our funeral home and guided them to the chapel. I opened the door for them, and they walked through the door, one by one, always connected by hands or chains. They made their way up the center of the chapel, and we stayed near the exit. My father didn't want anyone to disturb this time, or to accidentally walk into this room.

Their mom turned around and quickly stood up to greet Dom. When they got to the front of the room, the officers removed the shackles. He rubbed his wrists a few times and then opened his arms widely around his mom. She hugged him fiercely and they both began to cry together. She told him she loved him, and that she was thankful he was still with her. It seemed as if it had been a long time since they had seen each other. They held onto one another for a few long moments. It was both heartbreaking and heartwarming to witness.

Dom looked up towards the casket and his shoulders began to shake uncontrollably. He wiggled his way out of his mom's grasp and began to break down as he got closer and closer to the casket.

He began to cry so hard he was almost howling, louder than I had ever heard a coyote scream. He began yelling at his brother violently "WHY YOU? THIS SHOULD BE ME! NOT YOU!" He was sobbing and screaming so fiercely that I could see his spit flying across the casket. It gave me goosebumps.

His mother put her arm around him and tried to help calm him down. After a few minutes of continuous, heart wrenching moaning and crying he finally agreed to sit down.

The officers sat a few rows behind them and respected their need to grieve together as a family. After exactly one hour, the officers gently reminded Dom that it was time to leave.

Dom and his mother hugged once more before the officers put the shackles back on. They gently walked him towards the front of the building, as he was still quietly weeping, where the armored truck was already waiting for them. Two more armed men were waiting outside the truck and they all got in and drove away together in a flash.

At this time, I realized I had to get ready to go to school. I was going to be a little late, but the nuns at my school and my parents agreed that I could have a few minutes of leniency on busy funeral days.

Usually, on days like today I was thankful to have an escape from the funeral life. I would take my sweet time going home, make a few stops on the way, or spend a few extra minutes with friends to avoid having to go back to work straight away.

But today, I was on the edge of my seat waiting to get back. I couldn't wait to see what else would happen during this visitation.

I got home from school around 4:00 PM and the parking lot was filled with motorcycles. Every kind of motor bike you can think of! There were rows and rows of them. I had never seen anything like it! There were hundreds of men and women all wearing their gang vests smoking and drinking around the parking lot.

I began walking around the property trying to take it all in. It was like a parade of bikers surrounding the building! I was in awe of their outfits and their attitudes. And I was entertained by all of the strange looks I was getting from everyone around me. People were pointing towards me and asking each other why I was there!

As a reminder, I was 11 at this time. Not in high school, not in college. I was not even a teenager yet. Wearing my Catholic school uniform. No one could understand why a child my age would be skipping into a funeral home so nonchalantly. Those were some of my favorite moments from all the exotic funerals our family hosted. I loved confusing our visitors by my knowledge, experience, and comfort of all things death related at such a young age.

I pranced around the visitors outside and made my way towards the foyer. The moment I walked into the building I could tell that the day had been complete mayhem! A few things remained the same: my size, outfit, and comfort caught the attention of everyone in the room. All of the biker people turned their focus towards me. I began to get a little uncomfortable at this point. I decided to run upstairs to our apartment and find my black clothes so I could blend in a little better. I didn't want to draw attention, and I didn't want to miss out on the excitement.

A few minutes later I was dressed and went back downstairs. I sat in my father's office where I could look out of a massive window into our lobby. I felt protected and safe, but also had a full view of everything happening around me! It was thrilling to be so close to danger and yet, perfectly guarded.

I could see that everyone was packing a gun, there were tons of beards, long hair, big bellies, toned muscles and tattoos. Overall, they were a rough looking group of people. People that as an 11-year-old I would definitely avoid in all normal situations.

I had lost track of time and my father came in and sat down at his desk. He poured himself a drink and pulled out a cigarette. He only did that when he was almost done for the day, so I knew it had gotten late. He seemed stressed, but I was too concentrated on everything happening in the lobby to offer assistance. The manager, Scott, walked in and also grabbed a cigarette. From the sounds of it, they had definitely had an eventful day.

A few minutes after they arrived there was a knock on the door and the door began to open. It was quite a rude entrance, but after hearing what they had to say I could understand their eagerness to speak with my father.

"Mr. Lamb, I'm Officer Peterson, we just got word that a rival gang is on their way. We have called in backup and are blocking the parking lots at this moment. No one will be allowed in until we are sure the other gang is nowhere near the premises. As far as we are concerned, this wake ends now. We will make an announcement and tell everyone. We don't need any other deaths to result from this."

Scott chimed in and said "Why don't I go tell the family. It will be nicer for them to hear it from me, and then you can tell the people in the parking lot. They should be the first to get out since they're already in the parking lot. I can then slowly tell the visitors in the lobby, coffee room and chapel so we don't also cause chaos or destruction during an emotionally fragile time."

The officer agreed, and they both left right away.

The family was fine with the wake ending as it was already 9:00 PM. The funeral was set for the next day so there was nothing else left to do for the moment. They were tired and ready to end that long, emotional day.

The parking lot quickly emptied. And not just like: oh wow, that was faster than I expected – I'm talking LIGHTNING fast – hundreds of bikes, hundreds of people, all gone within eleven minutes. It's as if they already had exit strategies planned for times like this. It was all so perfectly executed. And no one got hurt. Quite the successful wake!

The next morning was Saturday. On a typical Saturday, I sleep in. But today, I woke up to the sound of hundreds of revving engines! You could hear them coming from a few blocks away. Maybe even a mile! Our parking lot attendants were out front, ready to line up two motorcycles at a time in two parallel lines so they could all easily drive together. Again, there were hundreds of them! They came from all over the country. It seemed as if there were even more people in attendance than the night before! They were all hugging, high-fiving, making random hand signals, maybe gang related, smoking and drinking, holding their holsters and their guns close by and donning their gang vests. It looked like there might have been some other gangs present as well to pay their respects because I didn't recognize their patches. I was sure I would have noticed them the night before.

I looked out my living room window over the parking lot and saw lines of bikes snaking back and forth in two parallel lines preparing for their big ride. It was exciting, and would have been more exciting to watch, like a parade, if it hadn't been for a funeral. But I didn't care, I wanted to watch it anyway!

I put on my black outfit, and even found a bedazzled black jacket to blend in with the bikers. I looked back out my living room window and saw police lights at every intersection I could see. They were prepared for the effect this would have on our local traffic and wanted to keep everything organized, light, and continuously moving to end the procession. The drive was about 20 minutes from the funeral home to the cemetery, so there were a lot of intersections that would be impacted! The drivers that morning would probably be infuriated, but also mesmerized by the long line of motorcycles they would witness on their morning drives.

The three of us, Dad, Scott, and I, rode in the first car behind the family in limos who were following the hearse with John's body. We had to be there early enough to help prepare for the funeral service before everyone else arrived.

Once we arrived, it took another 20 minutes for the rest of the entourage to assemble at the grave site. The police officers followed the bikers as they crossed each intersection to ensure there was enough coverage at the cemetery site as well. They were taking precautionary measures after the threat of a rival gang at the wake the day before.

The family took seats next to the grave and a sea of people swarmed around the grave site. By the time the service began, smoke had filled the air around us, bottles of whiskey were being sent around, and they were all shouting words that I couldn't clearly understand. It was probably better that way.

The Priest spoke as loudly as he could, but I doubt he could be heard by everyone. He was saying his prayers, and after a few minutes he motioned to Scott to begin lowering the casket into the grave. Once the final words were spoken, and the sign of the cross was made, one of the bikers raised his arm slowly above his head and shot his gun into the air. Once the first one went off, it felt and sounded as if fireworks were closing in on us! Everyone that had a gun pointed it straight up and shot one or two rounds towards the sky.

I jumped back and ran to my father. I was so frightened, I held him tight. It was such a shock! I was shaking and didn't know what to do or where to look so I hid my face in my father's coat. It was a terrifying noise and a horrifying situation to be in at my age. But Scott bent down to me and yelled over the shots that it was okay and assured me we wouldn't get hurt.


The police officers didn't even flinch! They knew that this was part of the tradition and allowed them to do so. Hundreds of guns, hundreds of shots, and no response whatsoever. It was bizarre to witness! It lasted only a few minutes, but it was longer than enough for me. To this day whenever I watch fireworks I still get chills that bring me back to this moment. It has definitely left a lasting impression.

When it was time to start moving and head back, I ran to the hearse. It's always the first car to go back to the funeral home, and at the end of the service it is empty. I was done with the biker gang and had seen enough!

I was told the next day that those hundreds of people stayed at the cemetery for hours drinking bottles of booze, shooting their guns, and smoking cartons of cigarettes!

They certainly gave a whole new meaning to the term "graveyard shift."

# CHAPTER 12

---

# The Noisy Neighbors

While you may think that the wakes and the funerals are the noisiest parts of this business, there's another side that I haven't exposed yet.

Embalming.

The embalmers have an incredibly fragile position as well. They are in charge of transforming the deceased's body back to a life-like look. It requires a lot of time, knowledge, and experience to be able to effectively take care of a lifeless human body. They have to go to school to understand which chemicals to use, how to apply them, and how to sometimes fix violent scars from death. It takes them years of studying to earn a degree.

I'll never forget my parents alma mater song to the tune of the Christmas classic song, *O Christmas Tree*

"We live for you, we die for you, National Embalming School.

And when you die, and go to sleep, we'll dig a hole, 'bout six feet deep.

We live for you, we die for you, National Embalming School!"

Talk about a sense of humor that is needed for this educational route!

Aside from their quirks, they have an incredibly challenging position because they are literally setting the stage for the final curtain call. This is the last time the living will view the deceased before burial or cremation. That's a lot of pressure, if you ask me.

Can you imagine waking up every day and knowing that today they will go into work and stand in a freezing cold room all day to prepare someone's body for their last days above ground. For the last time their loved ones will physically see them.

Usually, the embalmers are given a picture or two of the person at their happiest and they do their best to try and recreate that look to bring comfort to those who will miss this person in their lives. So, not only do they have to physically prepare the body, but they also need to know hair and makeup basics. They need to be able to match skin tones, hair colors, eyeshadows and lipstick shades to pictures, while making it all look lively.

And let me also add, they had some of the hardest jobs in relation to the ghosts on site.

If you asked me today if I had ever seen a ghost in any of the years I lived above a funeral home, I would say "aside from my brother wearing a sheet over his head and chasing me throughout the chapels, no I never saw a ghost while living above a funeral home."

And that's the honest truth.

I never saw a demon, a spirit, a shadow figure, nothing! I even wondered whether our souls follow our bodies once we die. I'm still not sure to this day.

However, although I never saw one, that doesn't mean I didn't hear any. And they were the loudest and the most destructive in the embalming room. But they weren't ghosts exactly. The noisy ones were poltergeists.

What's the difference? Well, I'm glad you asked.

Ghosts are apparitions of deceased individuals. They can scare us to death, and they can chill us to our bones, but there are several significant differences between ghosts and poltergeists.

Poltergeists are noisy and usually made up of energy. They can be responsible for physical disturbances such as loud noises and objects being moved or destroyed. It can feel like pure chaos is in the air, and there's nothing you can do about it.

Let me put it to you this way — The embalming room was like a 24 hour night club for poltergeists. The energy in that room caused so many disturbances that could be heard throughout the whole building! We'd have to make excuses for them such as air conditioning kicking in, repairs being done on pipes and so on.

I believe that because of how many bodies went in and out of that room that sometimes energy would stay long after the body had been removed and those energies would then band together to create massive happenings.

I noticed that these noisy occurrences usually happened when we were busier. The weeks where had a few more services than normal, when we were already exhausted, stressed, and agitated from working long, hard hours.

Go ahead, poltergeists, kick us while we're down! And while you're at it, clang away in the embalming room and scare us all half to death!

The winter was always the loudest time of the year. There are more natural deaths in the cold, so winter was usually our busier season of the year, which meant the poltergeists were large and in charge.

The embalmers had the brunt of the experiences. Towels would be thrown across the room, empty gurneys lined against the wall would be flipped over and slammed to the ground, water faucets would turn on by themselves at full blast, and lights would constantly flicker.

I remember one day I was delivering a body to the embalming room and as I approached the large door from the elevator I heard one of the embalmers, Eric, scream at the top of his lungs "STOP THIS NOW!" It almost sounded like he was scolding a misbehaving child.

"I don't have time to clean up after you! Stop acting like a pest! You can't just throw things around and expect them to pick themselves up! It is time to stop your childish ways and let me work!"

While I had my head pressed up against the thin opening so I could hear this interaction better, I began to laugh a little. I could imagine these poltergeists looking so smug and laughing to themselves seeing Eric lose his mind over the racket and annoyance. These poltergeists were the best pranksters, but could also become very distracting to someone who had to deal with them on a regular basis. Especially during busier times when we were all stressed, this would only make matters worse.

If the embalmers weren't happy, no one was happy! So we'd all have to deal with this poltergeist cycle where the embalmers would come, work, scream, finish, go home, and come back the next morning to total disarray in their workspace and scream some more. After a few weeks of this madness there would be quiet and peace for a while, and we would all appreciate the break from their disturbances.

While I never embalmed a body myself, the embalmers position taught me the importance of paying attention to details. And not just physical details, but the emotional details as well. Even though their focus is primarily on the physical status of a lifeless body, there are ways in which they can showcase the kind of person that body held.

You see, we are so much more than our physical bodies. Our minds, our souls, our interests, our beliefs, our values, and our cultures make us the person we truly are. It is not our limbs, the size of our foreheads, or the curve of our figures that dictate who we are. There is so much more beyond the surface that can dictate our true selves.

The poltergeists were always a problem.

Not just for the embalmers.

If you know anything about poltergeists, you know that their energy is violent, and it moves. It is transient. Which is terrifying in itself because if you have poltergeist activity in one area of your home, or your building, you have poltergeist activity EVERYWHERE.

That included our home. I can't explain it perfectly, but there were certain noises that you just knew weren't made by anyone living. Anyone in their right mind wouldn't think to make the kind of noises that poltergeists make.

They make startling noises that humans are incredibly frightful of. If living, breathing, humans made noises like this, I would assume that there was an underlying motivation. Maybe they would be trying to scare someone to death. You know my brother Matt, he might be one of those people. But, in a strange way, I felt that I knew his noises. Maybe better than I knew my own. I knew in my bones when he was really trying to scare me. Even if it worked because of the element of surprise, I believe that I could still sense when he was behind it.

Yes, there were other noises that I couldn't quite pinpoint the cause of. And these, I believe now, were the poltergeists making their presence known.

Not only because they were strange, blood curdling, terrifying noises out of nowhere and for no reason, but also because of the way our family dogs reacted.

Great Danes are not fearful dogs. They are monsters! Sweet and caring monsters, but still, they are fueled with brute force and strength behind their somewhat calm complexion.

It was as if the dogs had a sixth sense of their own. Right before a poltergeist would make themselves known the dogs would start barking in the direction that the sounds would eventually come from. They wouldn't be able to predict that with Matt.

One of the most memorable was when our Great Dane, Smokey, started barking at the living room china cabinet. I wondered what was triggering this response, at a silent china cabinet. And just a few moments later, I heard an eerie creaking noise, as if the china cabinet door was sinisterly opening.

I was naturally uncomfortable so I turned around to leave and as I walked into the kitchen I felt the hairs on the back of my neck begin to stand. I decided to curl myself into the corner of the countertop and sat there a few moments listening to the sound of my breath getting faster and faster.

Just then, it sounded as if hundreds of china dishes were shattering on the ground.

One of the loudest crashing noises I had ever heard. Smokey was barking uncontrollably and the whole apartment felt as if there was a hurricane of chaotic energy rushing around.

This went on for the longest thirty seconds of my life and I was frozen still for most of it.

I finally mustered up the courage to slowly stand up and peek around the corner of the kitchen into the living room. I was expecting to see the china cabinet fallen over, glass everywhere, and prayed that Smokey wasn't injured.

But when I looked around, there was nothing. There were no dishes on the ground, the cabinet wasn't even open. Smokey was laying perfectly still on the ground next to the couch on the opposite side of the room, and everything was fine. Except for my breath.

My breathing had graduated from heavy to hyperventilating. Even with the stillness in the room, the atmosphere was fueled by mayhem. I couldn't understand what was going on, and ran to my bedroom. Smokey followed.

The rest of the week, Smokey would bark at random furniture throughout the apartment, and I would freeze in shock from various shattering noises. Thankfully, nothing was ever broken.

Except for my terrified and fragile heart, of course.

# CHAPTER 13

---

# Closing the Casket

By now you've probably formed a pretty clear picture of my parents. You can gather the type of people they were, what their priorities were, and how they held themselves. They were hard core professionals all day, everyday, and they had the strongest work ethics I had ever experienced. Choosing to leave their youngest child at home to live above the funeral home as a teenager wasn't a light decision.

Yes, they wanted to move to the city so they could continue to build their professional reputations and expand their social lives, but they wouldn't have just let anyone live above the funeral home by themselves.

They trusted me.

They knew that if they let me live there I would continue with the same work ethic. I would care for their business that they built from basically the ground up. They knew that their reputation would be safe with me and that I would help keep

their business efficient and successful. Even while in high school.

I did just that.

And sure, I had my fun while doing it! I threw massive parties, chauffeured substantial amounts of beer in hearses across the city, made friends with mobsters, all while getting steady grades and participating in extracurricular activities such as cheerleading, volleyball, theatre, and whatever else I could get involved in, all without any parental supervision. It was a sweet life for the most part!

With all of that in mind, this experience gave me countless tools that I could rely on throughout my life because I was independent, responsible, mentally strong, organized, and could do a keg stand before taking a body to the embalming room.

Aside from giving me insane life experiences and great stories for a memoir, having this upbringing from birth also taught me a lot of lessons about life.

The employees of the funeral home were like my second family. They all treated me as if I was their own child, niece, or granddaughter. They checked in on me whenever we crossed paths and offered to assist me with everything from household issues, homework, and sometimes my overnight duties.

I often used to imagine what they would tell their families about their work at the funeral home. Everyone kind of has a general idea of what an undertaker is, or a funeral director as they'd prefer to be called, but they don't know what it takes to hold this position on a daily basis.

Every day they wake up to help families navigate some of the most difficult days of their lives. The shock and sadness of a recent death is still fresh, and sometimes it's so sudden that there are no plans or preparations in place to guide them. Taking on that sadness every single day takes a toll. It can become difficult to find happiness in other areas of their life when your focus is a tunnel vision towards death.

For some, it becomes a straightforward process. A business transaction. Everything from length of the visitation, color of the casket, floral display, prayer card design, required refreshments and more, to logistics for the funeral procession are discussed and decided in one or two meetings. By associating this interaction with a set step-by-step system the funeral directors can help to relieve emotional impact and keep them focused on what needs to be done to provide a high quality memorial experience. Additionally, this approach can provide a protective barrier for their mental well-being. It's not meant to come off as cold, and funeral directors get very good at keeping their genuine caring nature intact while keeping their clients focused on the details, but it is a daily struggle.

I think another aspect of this position that makes it such a challenging role is that they never know what to expect. They never know how the families will react or what they will want to incorporate into the visitation and funeral to pay their respects.

These few days that funeral directors work with the families are some of the most important parts of the grieving process. They're in the process of a huge transition, and the manner in which the families proceed through this experience will help dictate how their future continues after this loss.

I became a funeral director myself aside from working in public relations and those two positions together taught me that everyone deserves to be respectfully represented in death. Whether they were a criminal or the pope, everyone deserves a wake. It doesn't matter whether ten people show up, or a thousand people, because the wake isn't actually for the deceased. It is for the living. It is a chance to mourn and to gain closure.

We all grieve losses, and the way we share that grief with others is also important to process this transition. The stories we share with others and the stories we keep to ourselves help us keep our loved ones' memories alive. And while we all grieve differently whether it is at the top of a mountain all alone, or with a room full of people, everyone deserves an opportunity to face death. Everyone is entitled to a moment of release when they lose a loved one and taking that opportunity away from the living is unforgivable.

Funeral directors take an oath before they accept this path. They make a commitment to provide that opportunity for grieving, and to help those who are mourning design an experience to find closure and hope for the future. Their impact on our lives through these harsh realities is often life-changing without many of us realizing all of the effort and details that are taken into consideration.

So, as you can see, living and working in a funeral home may have had its own set of challenges, but I will never regret my childhood experiences because it has given me an amazing mindset to live my life.

There are a few mantras I have walked away from this business with:

Tell the people you love, that you love them all of the time.

- Drink the water, or drink the champagne.
- Don't let worry or regrets consume you.
- Take every opportunity you are given.
- And whatever happens in your life, good or bad, enjoy the process, and lay it to rest.

# ACKNOWLEDGEMENTS

Sheila Lamb-Gabler and her daughter, Rose Gabler, had a wonderful experience writing this book together. However, they didn't do it without the support of countless individuals who helped bring these stories to life.

Sheila here! And I would like to take a moment to thank my family, Michael, Rose and Stephen, Joe and Liz, and Matt and the loving memories of my late husband Joe Gabler, my parents, Rose and Matt Lamb, and my brother, Matt Lamb. Additionally, I would like to thank Mary Pat and Steve Gilboy for their constant encouragement throughout these years. To my friends who supported me through these experiences, Julie McNally and Ken Gill, Grace and Brian McDonough, Elaine and Dave Kindt, Meg and Scot Crowell, and Rosie Munizzo and Matt McDonald, thank you. Furthermore, I would like to quickly shout out all of the friends who passed through my home above the funeral home throughout our younger years for the memories that made this book as amazing as it is! And last, but not least, I would like to thank my daughter, Rose, for embarking on this adventure through my childhood. Your writing has transformed some of my favorite memories into entertaining and meaningful truths for our audiences across the globe.

Rose's turn! I would also love to thank my family and friends for their friendship, encouragement, and motivation to continue writing and to experiment with new perspectives and styles of writing. I would like to also thank my mom, Sheila, for allowing me the opportunity to adapt your stories and experiences into this book. Your stories have changed the lives of so many, and it is an honor to be able to expand their reach and their impact through the written word. This journey has shaped my personal life in so many ways and I can only imagine how these memories will continue to influence hope in the lives of others for years to come!

# ABOUT THE AUTHORS

Sheila Lamb-Gabler grew up on the South Side of Chicago in a family that owned a funeral business. These foundational years impacted her way of living and empowered her to live life to the absolute fullest. She has certainly spread her wings throughout her life as she has transitioned from the funeral home  business to fulfilling her purpose through art and culture. She has visited over 60 countries and become a citizen of the U.A.E. Additionally, she has sat on many school and hospital boards across the globe and received several internationally-renowned awards for peace activism including Woman of the Year from the Mrs. Globe Foundation and the Humanitarian Award from Matter NGO.

As an Artist, Entrepreneur, and Event Expert, her global career has allowed her to connect with other cultures on the topic of peace through artistic expression. Seeing as creativity is now a core value of the Lamb and Gabler families, she was inspired to finally share her childhood experiences after the publication of her daughter's latest book. Sheila's mission has been fueled by her core values surrounding life and death with hopes to inspire others to live their lives fully and genuinely, while having as much fun as possible, of course! She is currently living in the Chicagoland area and often supports others who are struggling to discover methods to heal.

Rose Gabler is an Author and Creativity Coach. Growing up in a family of artists, she felt pressure to be artistically expressive but didn't know how to connect her innate creative strengths with her desired business goals. She began a lifelong journey trying to bridge this gap and faced many challenges in discovering a solid link.

After acquiring her master's degree in Business of Arts and Culture, traveling the world for three years, and interviewing hundreds of people in various industries about creativity, she discovered that there were five universal contributing factors that empower our ability to be creative and to utilize it as a skill. She was recently named one of the "Top 20 Female Entrepreneurs to Look For in 2021" and her newest book "The Creativity Gene: 5 Universal Traits to Spark Success" achieved best seller status in the first day.

Now, she lives in Chicago, Illinois. working with entrepreneurs, artists, and knowledge sharers to write books that will make the world a better place. "Laid to Rest" is her first biographical book.

CONSTANCE LOPEZ

# THE
# WINTER
# PRINCE

ONCE UPON A PRINCE

A BEAUTY AND THE BEAST RETELLING

**Once Upon A Prince**

The Unlucky Prince by Deborah Grace White

The Beggar Prince by Kate Stradling

The Golden Prince by Alice Ivinya

The Wicked Prince by Celeste Baxendell

The Midnight Prince by Angie Grigaliunas

The Poisoned Prince by Kristin J. Dawson

The Silver Prince by Lyndsey Hall

The Shoeless Prince by Jacque Stevens

The Silent Prince by C. J. Brightley

The Crownless Prince by Selina R. Gonzalez

The Awakened Prince Alora Carter

The Winter Prince by Constance Lopez

*__Grab the whole Once Upon A Prince series today!__*